1972

3 0301 00009978 4

PRINCIPLES OF CARTESIAN PHILOSOPHY

BARUCH SPINOZA

PRINCIPLES

OF

CARTESIAN PHILOSOPHY

Newly translated from the Latin
by HARRY E. WEDECK

With a Preface by DAGOBERT D. RUNES

PHILOSOPHICAL LIBRARY
New York

Library of Congress Catalog Card No. 60–53160

Printed in the United States of America

CONTENTS

PREFACE

Baruch Spinoza, the Dutch rabbi without congregation, was often referred to as the thinker of finalities. He did not hesitate to step where Descartes had hesitated and where his religious teachers turned back.

Spinoza declared when others hinted, and raised his voice to a clamor when others dared little more than whisper. He thus drew the brunt of orthodoxy in attack upon himself and became the anti-Christ of seventeenth-century Europe, that grand epoch which marked the end of Scholasticism and the dawn of the Enlightenment. He walked the crimson path of martyrdom, bevenomed by Christians, denounced by his kinsmen and denied even by his early admirers, who, though sparked by his brilliance, fled in fear of its inherent danger.

The flame of Spinozism shone across the lands of Europe, cold and cutting to the bigots, an inspiration to those spiritually yearning in the chains of traditional circumspection.

For a hundred years Spinoza slept the slumber of oblivion following the nightmare of persecution. Then in the years of the American and the French Revolutions the tortured spirit of the lonely rabbi was lifted from its darkness to the summit of philosophical esteem by the hands of such men as Goethe, Herder, Shelley, Lessing and others.

Baruch Spinoza was born in 1632, a small merchant's son, in Amsterdam, the "New Jerusalem" of that day. His father, a crypto-Jew, had fled the latter-day Inquisition of Portugal to found a new home in Holland. Hundreds of his kinsmen had taken sail to the same protective harbor in order to renew the practice of their ancient faith, which they had denied under threat and terror.

For some, life as pseudo-Catholics had lasted too long and even such zealots as Rabbi Isaak Uziel (died 1622) could not completely eradicate its traces. Uziel's successors, Rabbis Saul Levi Morteira, Isaak Aboab da Fonseca, and the tireless Menasseh ben Israel—whose work of talmudic "reconciliation" dominated the Amsterdam rabbinical school which sent a formidable new generation of Jewish teachers and scholars into the world—were deeply grounded in Torah, Talmud and Kabalah, the three fountainheads of Israel.

In this rabbinical school the young Spinoza received his training. In early years he was informed of the many attempts by Jews and Protestants alike to demythologize the Torah, to discredit the Talmud and to disparage the Kabalah.

Spinoza was an eager student and, as visitors to his home reported, a respected one, but in adolescence he seems already to have been inclined towards skepticism. He was not satisfied with Rabbi ben Israel's efforts to "even out" discrepancies and contradictions within the Bible and the Talmud and he rejected vehemently the numerology, word play and miracle lore of the Kabalah. He attached himself strongly, however, to the profound spirituality of the Kabalah, its cardinal concept of God being the *Ain Soph*—the Endless One—Whose Eternal Being (*Elohim*) lives in the soul of man (*Shekinah*). The

Kabalistic mystic teaching that man's love of God and man's love to man are one and the same thing is found time and again in Spinoza's profound "Man can be a God to Man."

The Kabalistic concept of the *Zaddik,* the Sage, who lives a life of perfection guided only by reason, justice and generosity, is close to Spinoza's "Free Man" who like a tower in the wind is not subject to the great avarices, greed, lust and glory, but lives rather in equanimity and security, forever conscious of the idea of God or Creative Nature (*Tikkun*).

As his library and correspondence indicate, Spinoza was well acquainted with the Hebrew philosophies of Ibn Ezra, Maimonides, Gersonides, Chasdai Crescas, Leo Abravanel and others. His statements on seeing the world *sub specie aeternitatis* can be traced directly to the medieval Hebraists.

While Spinoza's father was alive, the young theologian seemed to have constrained his rising opposition to traditionalism. In 1654 Michael Spinoza died. In 1656 Baruch Spinoza was expelled from the Amsterdam synagogue, largely because of the pressure of the Christian community.

Looking for a way to earn his living, Spinoza became a tutor in Hebrew at the Latin College of Franciscus Affinius van den Enden, a runaway Jesuit, natural scientist and dedicated Cartesian. Spinoza's friendship with van den Enden was of decisive influence upon his career. Rapidly the young tutor acquired Latin, history and mathematics; he became so proficient in the latter that he commenced a textbook on algebra.

We have a number of books and projects from this period in Spinoza's life, set down for his students: an *Apologia* in Spanish concerning his faith (this manu-

3

script, as well as the pages on algebra, are still undis-covered); an essay on the improvement of the mind; a Hebrew grammar (fragmentary); a book on God; and the present presentation of Descartes's philosophical principles and metaphysics.

Spinoza eagerly absorbed the philosophy of Descartes. Here he found a man after his own mind, a doubter, a searcher, a breaker of tradition. He became one of the many bright young followers of the grandiose Frenchman, who also had fled to Holland for sanctuary.

But contrary to Descartes, Spinoza had no room in his universe for a Church God besides God the Substance, nor for the concept of sin based on the premise of what he considered nonexistant, "free will." To Spinoza there was no good nor evil except in man's mind; no free will, only awareness of an act.

Virtue to him was its own reward; God, or *natura naturans,* not a punishing Lord but *ens perfectissimum,* the Ever-Being, acting according to timeless laws. To Spinoza the sinner was only a fool and the virtuous and free man a sage, since the greatest good leads also to the greatest happiness. Therefore the most ethical deed is to be most selfish in realizing one's inner self. Self-preservation is the Way to Virtue, and happiness a guide to self-improvement. Supreme Egoism is Egoism Supreme. To live by desire is the highest form of ethical conduct, but desire that springs from reason and not from confusion or affectations.

Spinoza did not come to Descartes empty-handed. He came with a mind full of ancient Hebrew wisdom and a strong wish to break with the morbid past and the presence of a Scholastic Europe. Descartes became his teacher and leader, but he went beyond the earth-shaking Frenchman deep into the finalities of One God and One

Soul experiencing its essence in union with Him, dedicated to a life of reason, kindness and devotion.

* * *

Only in a few instances did Spinoza cite exact quotations from the writings of Descartes. He added brief explanations to the latter's axioms strongly supporting the point of view that in his mind not all was axiomatic with the Cartesian axioms, indicating that Spinoza would rather have seen some of them presented as propositions.

There is no doubt that in the given era of seventeenth-century Europe the mathematical investigation of philosophical *themata* by means of axioms, definitions and postulates seemed to hold the key to certainty. However, Spinoza did not concur in Descartes' limitation of knowledge by the confines of its procedure, nor did he accede to Descartes' hidden postulates of Divine Providence beyond the finite substances of mind and matter with man acting out in free will within them.

Rather, Spinoza admitted to only one substance, *natura naturans* or Creative Nature, which man in his limitations conceives under two infinite attributes—namely, mind and matter—but which in reality does perexist (*substantia*) in innumerable attributes of which only these two are within man's vision.

Consequently, this Infinite Substance is not a creation of God but God Himself in His creative process, and man's so-called free will is no more than awareness of being driven in a certain direction among the oceanic motions of existence. In the words of Goethe, "One thinks he is pushing whilst being pushed."

* * *

5

I personally think that the illustrious Frenchman was not unaware of his self-imposed dualism but that he decided in view of the distressing cultural scene of his time to let caution be his guide.

Descartes paid homage to the Church and even managed to reach the protecting hand of Cardinal Mazarin. Learning of Galileo's predicament, the philosopher offered to the pyre his *Du Monde,* based on Copernican theories. Descartes was not the man to go the way of Giordano Bruno, who was burned alive in Rome in 1600 for saying what Descartes avoided.

Spinoza too was hesitant about writing the present work, lest his intimate personal views penetrate the cautious Cartesian structure and betray what his later works propounded. I am almost sure that these final thoughts were not unknown to Descartes, though hidden in the depths of his heart.

The dichotomy of Cartesian Catholicism was so deep that his contemporaries, Catholics and Protestants alike, with a few important exceptions, rejected, derided and persecuted him.

After a youth spent in a Jesuit college and dedicated mainly to mathematics, he refused to submit to the burdensome academic discipline of the world of Scholasticism and took up a career as mercenary soldier in various armies. After a brief return to Paris, he left for a freer Holland, where, like Spinoza, he led a life dedicated to philosophy and its liberation from the Scholastic yoke.

Even there he was subject to Church harassment, both Catholic and Protestant, and moved his domicile almost twenty times. In fact, he once had to appeal to the Prince of Orange for protection. The leader of a large Calvinist group in Holland, the Rector of the University of Utrecht, Gisbertus Voetius, had his writing banned and urged book burning and severe punishment.

In 1663, only thirteen years after Descartes's death, his books were placed on the Papal Index and in 1671 the teaching of his philosophy was prohibited at the University of Paris.

It is interesting to note that in the following centuries this very system of Cartesian reasoning was employed by Catholic critics to attack the theories of Spinoza, who in his later years threw off the saving discretion of his much admired teacher and spelled out the secret dreams of Descartes.

With his unresolved "dualism," his gentle obeisance to Rome and his indulgence of a bit of illogical voluntarism, Descartes, the dedicated mathematician and founder of analytical geometry, managed to head a gigantic wave of rationalism that finally broke the Scholastic bastions of Europe.

No man has done so much to free the mind of modern man as this René Descartes. His influence can be compared only with the impact of Charles Darwin in the nineteenth century.

In his lifetime and during the following centuries school after school closed its doors to the thoughts of this ungainly little bearded man, but man's yearning for truth, once detected or even envisioned, was touched by the greatness of Cartesianism, its elevation of reason to competence and of doubt as the sole gate to knowledge.

And what held good for Cartesianism was relevant equally to Spinozism, its final consequence. The pillorying of Descartes and of Spinoza placed their teaching in the focus of studious attention and the *impies novateurs* became the advance guard of a new world.

The casual reader may perhaps wonder how such

7

remote essays as those before us here could have had the great and liberating effects they did. Let him be reminded of the primitiveness of ancient weapons such as wooden catapults and battering rams with which whole cities and civilizations were conquered.

Descartes and Spinoza represent the best in intellectual leadership in critical times when a minor deviation from Scholastic Aristotelianism could and did lead to a kind of Church inquisitiveness that was a deterrent to all but a few.

* * *

The work before us appeared in Latin in 1663 carrying Spinoza's name as author, the only book published during his lifetime under his name. It was almost immediately translated into Dutch, indicating the wide popularity Descartes and Spinoza enjoyed, even in nonacademic circles.

Spinoza was assisted in its preparation by his tutor and later teaching associate, Franciscus Affinius van den Enden, and his friend Lodewijk Meyer, a physician and poet.

DAGOBERT D. RUNES

PART I

INTRODUCTION

Before entering upon the propositions themselves and their proofs, it seemed fitting to offer a succinct explanation why Descartes questioned everything, in what manner he discovered the firm foundations of knowledge, and finally by what means he freed himself from all his doubts. All this matter we should certainly have reduced to a mathematical orderliness, had we not considered the prolixity necessary for its presentation a hindrance for a proper understanding of the entire subject that ought to be viewed, as in the case of a picture, by a comprehensive survey.

Descartes, then, proceeding with the utmost caution in the investigation of nature, attempted:

1. to reject all pre-conceived notions;
2. to find the bases for all necessary superstructures;
3. to discover the cause of error;
4. to understand everything clearly and distinctly.

In order to attain the first, second, and third objectives, he proceeds to question everything; not indeed as a skeptic, for whom the final end is nothing but doubt, but with a view to freeing his mind from all pre-conceptions and hence to discover ultimately the solid and irrefutable bases of knowledge that he could not fail to discover, if such exist. For the true principles of knowledge must be so lucid and convincing that they require no proof, exclude all risk of doubt, and make any proof impossible without them. After prolonged doubt, Descartes discovered such principles. Upon their discovery, it was not difficult for him to distinguish truth from falsity, to discover the cause of error, and furthermore to take precautions not to assume what is false and doubtful as truth and certainty.

To reach the fourth and last objective, that is, to understand clearly and distinctly, his principal rule was to review all the simple ideas, of which all the others are composed, and to examine them severally. For if he could perceive simple ideas clearly and distinctly, he would doubtless understand all the other ideas composed of these simple ones, with the same clarity and perspicuity. With these preliminary remarks, we shall briefly explain how Descartes called everything into question, found the true principles of knowledge, and liberated himself from the difficulties of doubt.

Universal Doubt

First of all he considers all things perceived by the senses, namely: heaven, earth, and such notions, and even his own person; all these things he had until then believed to exist in the scheme of Nature. And he doubts their certainty, because his own senses had sometimes deceived him and in his dreams had often convinced him that many things really had an objective existence that he had afterward discovered to be illusory; and finally because he had heard others, even in waking moments, assert that they felt pain in limbs that they had long since lost. Therefore it was not without reason that he was able to doubt the existence even of his own body.

From all these circumstances he was able to deduce rightly that the senses were not a very strong foundation on which to build the superstructure of all knowledge—for they can be called in question—but that certainty depends on other, more convincing principles. To pursue such speculations further, he next considers all the universals, such as material nature in general and its extent, likewise shape, quantity, and so on, and also all the mathematical truths. Although these ideas seemed to him more convincing than all those that he had experienced by the sense, he still found a reason for doubting them; since others too had been mistaken about them, and particularly since a certain old notion had been implanted in his mind that a God existed, all-powerful, by whom he had been created just as he was, and who had perhaps made it possible for him to be deceived about those ideas that seemed very clear to him. By this means he questioned everything.

Discovery of the Basis of All Knowledge

To discover the true principles of knowledge, he investigated next whether he had called into question everything that could come within his thought: thus he would examine whether there was not something left perhaps that he had not yet doubted. If indeed he found anything, by such a method of doubting, that could not be called in question for any of the preceding reasons, or for any other reason, he rightly considered that he could accept it as a basis on which to build the superstructure of all his knowledge. And although he now appeared to doubt everything—for he had doubted equally both the notions

11

that he had received through the senses, and those that he perceived through comprehension only—still there was something left to be examined, namely, himself who doubted thus; not in so far as he was composed of a head, hands, and other members of the body, all matters of doubt; but only in so far as he doubted, thought, and so on.

After a careful examination, he realized that he could entertain doubt on this point for none of the previously mentioned reasons. For, whether the thinking process persists in sleep or in wakefulness, he still thinks and is; whether others were in error about other subjects, or even himself, none the less they existed, since they were in error. Nor could he imagine any author of his own nature, however cunning, who could deceive him in this regard; for it must be granted that he himself existed as long as he supposed himself to be deceived. Finally, whatever other cause for doubt might be conceived, none could be adduced that did not at the same time make him overwhelmingly certain of his own existence. Furthermore, adducing more reasons for doubt meant adducing also more proofs to convince him of his own existence. So much so, that wherever he turned to doubt, he was none the less constrained to exclaim: *I doubt, I think, therefore I am.*

With the discovery of this truth he likewise found the basis of all the sciences; and even a standard and rule for all the other truths, namely: *Whatever is perceived as clearly and distinctly as this truth is true.*

That no other basis for knowledge than this is possible is abundantly and more than sufficiently clear from what has preceded, since all the other notions can most readily be called in question, but this one cannot be questioned in any manner whatever. However, in regard to this principle, it must first of all be observed that the statement *I doubt, I think, therefore I am* is not a syllogism, whose major premise has been omitted. For, if it were a syllogism, the premises ought to have been clearer and better known than the conclusion itself, *therefore I am*: and so *I am* would not be the first basis of all knowledge; besides, it would not be a certain conclusion, for its truth would depend on universal premises that the author had long since called in question. So *I think, therefore I am* is a single proposition, equivalent to this one: *I am a thinking being.*

Furthermore, to avoid confusion in what follows (for the matter must be perceived clearly and distinctly), we must understand what we are. For, once this is clearly and distinctly understood, our being will not be confused with others. To deduce this therefore from what precedes, our author thus continues.

He recalls in memory all the thoughts that he once had regarding himself: that his soul was a subtle body similar to wind, fire, or air, pervading the thicker parts of the body; that his body was more familiar to him than his soul, and that he had a clearer and more distinct perception of it. He found that all this was manifestly at variance with what he had until then understood. For it was possible for him to doubt his body, but not his existence in so far as he could think. Moreover, not perceiving this clearly or distinctly, he consequently had to reject it as false, according to the method that he had proposed for himself. Hence, since he could not, considering what he already knew of himself, recognize the relation of these questions to himself, he proceeded to investigate further what properly belonged to his being, what he had been unable to doubt, and on account of which he was forced to affirm his existence.

13

Such are the following notions: *He must beware of self-deception; he wanted to comprehend many concepts; he questioned everything that he could not comprehend; up to this time he had posited one truth only; he denied everything else, rejecting it as false; even in spite of himself he imagined many things; finally, he observed many things that appeared to come from the senses.* Since, equally evidently, his existence rested on each one of these assertions and since he was unable to view any one of them as among the ideas that he had questioned, and finally since they could all be conceived under the same attribute, it followed that they were all truths and belonged to his nature. And so, in saying *I think*, he understood all these modes of thought: *doubt, understanding, affirmation, denial, wishing, not wishing, imagination, and feeling.*

It must first of all be observed—and this will be very useful in what follows, where the distinction between mind and matter is discussed:

1st. These modes of thought are clearly and distinctly comprehended without other questions that are still in doubt.

2nd. The clear and distinct concept that we have of these modes of thought is rendered obscure and confused, if we wish to add to them something that still remains in doubt.

Release from All Doubts

Finally, to reach assurance on what he had questioned and to remove all doubt, he proceeded to inquire into the nature of the most perfect Being and on its existence. For, upon discovering the existence of a most perfect

Being, by whose power all things are produced and conserved, and whose nature refutes the possibility of his being an impostor, the reason for doubt, that he entertained through his ignorance of his true cause, will be eliminated. For he will know that the faculty of distinguishing the true from the false was not given to him by a God supremely good and veracious to produce deception. And so the mathematical truths and all those things that appear very evident to him will not admit of any suspicion whatever. Then he advances a step forward to eliminate the other causes of doubt and inquiries: How does it happen that we are sometimes mistaken? When he discovered that this arises from our own use of free will in giving assent even to what we perceived only confusedly, he was at once able to conclude that he could avoid error in the future, provided he gave assent to clear and distinctive perceptions only. Each one may easily achieve this of his own accord, since he has the power of restraining his will and confining it within the limits of the understanding. But as, in early youth, we acquire many preconceptions from which we are not easily liberated, he proceeds, in order to free us so that we accept nothing that we do not clearly and distinctly perceive, to review all the simple notions and ideas, of which all our thoughts are composed; to examine each one separately, in order to discover whatever is obscure in each of them. Thus he will be in a position to make an easy distinction between what is clear and what is obscure, and from clear and distinct thoughts, and so to discover easily the real distinction between the soul and the body: what is clear and what is obscure in the perceptions that we experience by the senses; and lastly, the difference between sleep and wakefulness. Thereupon, he could no longer doubt his wakeful periods or be deceived by the sense; and thus he

15

emancipated himself from all the doubts previously considered.

But, before I stop at this point, I must, it appears, give a satisfactory reply to those who argue as follows: Since the existence of God is not known to us by itself, it does not seem that we can ever be certain of anything: nor will the existence of God ever be known to us. For from uncertain premises (and we saw that everything is uncertain as long as we are unaware of our origin) no certainty can be reached.

To resolve this difficulty, Descartes replies thus: From the fact that we do not yet know whether perhaps the author of our origin has treated us such as to be deceived, even in what appears to us most evident, we cannot in the slightest degree doubt what we know clearly and distinctly by itself, or by reasoning, so long as we give our attention to it; we can doubt only what we previously proved to be true, the memory of which can recur, when we no longer regard the reasons that led to these conclusions and which we have forgotten. Therefore, although the existence of God can be known not by itself but only by some other thing, we shall still be able to attain positive knowledge of God's existence, provided we pay the most careful attention to all the premises from which we draw this conclusion. See *Principles*, Part I, article 13, and the *Response to the Two Objections*, No. 3 and the end of the *Fifth Meditation*.

But, since this reply does not satisfy certain questioners, I shall offer another one. We have seen in the preceding arguments, when we spoke of the certainty and the evidence of our existence, that we reached this conclusion from the fact that, in whatever direction we turned our mental gaze, we encountered no reason for doubt that did not assure us, by that very fact, of our existence;

whether we considered our own nature, or whether we imagined the author of our nature as a cunning impostor, or finally whether we appealed to any other reason for doubt outside ourselves; a condition that we never hitherto found present in any other matter. For, although, if we consider the nature of, for example, the Triangle, we are forced to conclude that its three angles are equal to two right angles, we cannot however draw the same conclusion from the fact that perhaps we are deceived by the author of our nature: whereas we thus reached the most certain conclusion of our existence. Therefore we are not forced to conclude, wherever we turn our mental gaze, that the three angles of a Triangle are equal to two right angles, but on the contrary we find a reason for doubt, because we have no idea of God such as to make us think it is impossible for God to be an impostor. For it is just as easy for one who does not have a true idea of God, that we now suppose we do not have, to conceive his author as an impostor or as not an impostor: just as, for the person who has no idea of a Triangle, it is as easy to conceive its three angles as equal or as not equal to two right angles.

Hence we grant that, apart from our existence, we cannot be absolutely certain of anything, however carefully we consider its demonstration, so long as we have no clear and distinct conception of God that obliges us to declare that God is supremely veracious, just as the idea that we have of the Triangle forces us to conclude that its three angles are equal to two right angles; but we deny that we cannot on that account attain a knowledge of anything. For, as is clear from all that has just been said, the crux of the entire question rests on this point only: that we can form a concept of God that does not induce us to conceive him, equally well, as being an impostor, but that forces us to affirm that he is supremely veracious. For as soon as we form such an idea, the reason for doubting the mathematical truths is removed. For, wherever we turn our mental gaze, to question any of these truths, we shall encounter nothing from which we ought not to conclude that this truth is quite certain, as in the case of our existence. For example, if, after attaining the idea of God, we carefully consider the nature of the Triangle, this idea will compel us to assert that its three angles are equal to two right angles; but if we consider the idea of God, it will force us to assert that he is supremely veracious, the author and the continuous preserver of our nature and hence does not deceive us in regard to this truth respecting the Triangle.

It will be no less impossible for us to think, on considering the idea of God (that we assume we have now discovered), that he is an impostor than, on considering the idea of the Triangle, to think that its three angles are not equal to two right angles. And, just as we can form such an idea of a Triangle, although we do not know whether the author of our nature is deceiving us, so we can also make the idea of God clear to us and set it before our gaze, although doubtful at the same time whether the author of our nature deceives us in all respects. And, provided we have this idea, however we may have acquired it, it will be sufficient, as has now been shown, to remove all doubt. Having predicated what has just been said, I now answer the difficulty that has been raised: we cannot be certain about anything—not indeed, so long as we are ignorant of the existence of God (for I have not spoken of this)—but so long as we have no clear and distinct idea of him. Therefore, if anyone wishes to dispute with me, his argument will have to be as follows: We can be certain of nothing until we have a clear and distinct idea of God. But we cannot have a clear and distinct idea of God, so long as we do not know whether the author of our nature deceives us. Therefore we cannot be certain about anything so long as we do not know whether the author of our nature deceives us, and so on. To this I reply by granting the major premise, and denying the minor premise. For we have a clear and distinct idea of the Triangle, although we do not know whether the author of our nature deceives us; and, providing we have such an idea of God as I have just shown at great length, we shall be capable of doubting neither his existence, nor any mathematical truth. With these preliminary remarks, we now approach the exposition itself.

DEFINITIONS

I. By the term *thought* I comprehend all that is in us and of which we are immediately conscious.

Thus all the operations of the will, understanding, imagination, and of the senses are thoughts. But I have added immediately, *to exclude those things that are the consequences of thoughts; thus voluntary motion has thought as a principle, but is not itself a thought.*

II. By the term *idea* I understand that form of any thought whatever by the immediate perception of which I am conscious of the thought itself.

Thus I can explain nothing in words, when I understand what I say, without its being certain thereby that there is in me the idea of what is signified by these words. And so I do not call ideas those images only depicted in imagination; rather, I do not call them ideas at all, in as much as they are in the corporeal imagination, that is, depicted in some part of the brain, but only in so far as they inform the mind itself that is directed to that part of the brain.

19

III. By *the objective* reality* of an idea I understand the entity of the thing represented by the idea, in so far as this entity is in the idea.

In the same way me may say objective perfection, objective artifice, *and so on. For whatever we perceive in the objects of the ideas is objectively in the ideas themselves.*

IV. The same things are said to be *formally** in the objects of the ideas, when they are in them such as we perceived them; and *eminently,* when they are not indeed such, but so great that they can take the place of such as are.

Note, when I say that the cause eminently *contains the perfections of its effect, then I want to signify that the cause contains the perfections of the effect more excellently than the effect itself contains them.* See also Axiom 8.

V. Everything in which there dwells immediately, as in a subject, or by which something exists that we perceive, that is, some property or quality or attribute, whose real idea is in us, is called *Substance.*

We have no other idea of the Substance itself, precisely considered, except that it is a thing in which exists formally* and eminently this something that we perceive or which is objectively* in one of our ideas.

VI. The substance in which thought exists immediately is called *Mind.*

I speak here of Mind rather than of Soul, since the term Soul is ambiguous and is often used for a corporeal object.

VII. The substance that is the immediate subject of

---

* Spinoza's use of "objective" corresponds to our use of "subjective." In IV, "formally" corresponds to our use of "objectively." Translator's note.

extension and of the accidents that presuppose extension, as shape, position, spatial motion, and so on, is called *Body*.

There will have to be a later investigation whether the substance that is called Mind and Body is one and the same substance, or whether they are two different substances.

VIII. The substance which we understand to be supremely perfect in itself, and in which we conceive absolutely nothing that involves some defect or a limitation of perfection, is called *God*.

IX. When we say that some attribute is contained in the nature or concept of a thing, it is the same as if we said that this attribute is true of this being, or can be truly affirmed of it.

X. Two substances are said to be really distinguished when each one can exist without the other.

We have omitted here the postulates of Descartes, because we draw no conclusions from them in what follows; however, we seriously ask our readers to read them and carefully meditate on them.

AXIOMS

I. We attain knowledge and certainty of an unknown thing only through knowledge and certainty of another thing that is itself anterior in certainty and knowledge.

II. Reasons are postulated that make us doubt the existence of our bodies.

This has been forcefully established in the Introduction, and for this reason is presented here as an axiom.

III. If we have anything beyond Mind and Body, it is less known to us than Mind and Body.

Note that these axioms affirm nothing about things exterior to us, but only what we find in ourselves, in so far as we are thinking beings.

PROPOSITION I

We can be absolutely certain of nothing so long as we do not know that we exist.

PROOF

This proposition is self-evident. For a person who does not know absolutely that he exists does not know either that he is an affirming or denying being, that is, that he affirms or denies with certainty.

At this point it must be observed that, although we affirm and deny many things with great certainty without regard to the fact of our existence, nevertheless, everything could be called in question, unless this were first posited as an indubitable fact.

PROPOSITION II

"I am" must be known by itself.

PROOF

If it is denied, it will then not become known except by another thing, the knowledge (*by Axiom* 1) and the certainty of which will be anterior in us to this affirmation: *I am*. But that is absurd (*by the preceding proposition*); therefore *I am* must be known by itself.

Q.E.D.

PROPOSITION III

I am *is not the first truth and is not known by itself, in so far as I am a thing consisting of a body.*

PROOF

There are certain reasons that make us doubt the existence of our body (*by Axiom* 2), therefore (*by Axiom* 1) we shall not reach certainty in regard to it, except through the knowledge and certainty of something else, that is itself anterior in knowledge and certainty. Therefore this affirmation *I am* is not the first truth and is not known by itself in so far as *I am* a thing formed of a body.   Q.E.D.

PROPOSITION IV

I am cannot be the first truth known, except in so far as we think.

PROOF

This affirmation *I am a corporeal thing or formed of a body* is not the first known truth (*by the preceding proposition*) ; nor am I certain even of my own existence, in as much as I am composed of some thing other than mind and body: for if we are formed of some other thing, different from mind and body, this thing is less known to us than the body (*by Axiom* 3) : therefore *I am* cannot be the first known truth, except in so far as we think.

Q.E.D.

COROLLARY

Hence it is evident that the mind or the thinking thing is more known than the body.

But for a fuller explanation read the Principles, Part I, articles 11 and 12.

SCHOLIUM

Each person perceives with the greatest certainty that he affirms, denies, doubts, understands, imagines, and so on; or, that he exists as doubting, understanding, affirming, and so on; or, in a word, as *thinking*; nor can he call this in question. Therefore this affirmation, *I think*, or *I am a thinking being* is the sole and most certain basis of all philosophy (*by Proposition* 1), and since in the sciences, to acquire most certainty about things, the only thing to be sought and desired is to deduce everything as clear and distinct as the principles from which they were deduced, it manifestly follows that everything that is as evident to us and all that we perceive as clearly and distinctly as this principle of ours that has already been established, and all that coincides with this principle and depends on it so that, if we wanted to doubt it, it would be necessary to doubt this principle also, must be accepted as an ultimate truth. But, to proceed with the utmost caution possible in enumerating these things, I shall first of all admit as equally evident and perceived by us as clearly and distinctly only those things that each person observes in himself or in so far as he is a thinking being. As, for example, that he wishes this or that, that he has such and such assured ideas, and that one idea contains in itself more reality and perfection than another idea;

hus the idea that objectively the entity and the perfec-
ion of the substance are far more perfect than the idea
hat contains only the objective perfection of some acci-
lent; that idea finally is the most perfect of all that is the
dea of the supremely perfect being. We perceive these
hings, I assert, not only with equal evidence and equal
larity, but perhaps even more distinctly. For not only do
hey affirm that we think but also the manner of our
hinking.

Furthermore, we shall also say that those things agree
vith this principle that cannot be called in question, un-
ess at the same time this unshakable basis is also called
n question. As for example, if anyone wants to doubt
vhether something can be produced from nothing, he
vill at the same time be able to doubt whether we exist
s long as we think. For if I can affirm something from
10thing, namely, that it can be the cause of something,
shall be able, with equal justification, to affirm thought
rom nothing and say that I am nothing while I think.
ince this is impossible for me, it will also be impossible
or me to think that something comes from nothing.

After these considerations, I have decided to set forth
ere in the proper order those principles that now seem
o us necessary, so that we may advance further and add
hem to the number of axioms, since they are proposed
s Axioms by Descartes, at the end of the *Responses to
he Second Objections*, and I do not want to be more
igorous than myself. However, in order not to diverge
rom the order already begun, I shall try to clarify them
s far as possible and to show how they depend on each
ther, and how they all depend on this principle *I am a
hinking being* or agree with it through evidence and
eason.

25

AXIOMS
Taken from Descartes

IV. There are different degrees of reality or entity: for the substance has more reality than the accident or the mode; and the infinite substance more than the finite; and so there is more objective reality in the idea of the substance than in that of the accident, and in the idea of the infinite substance than in the idea of the finite substance.

This axiom is known from contemplation alone of our ideas, of whose existence we are certain, since they are modes of thought: for we know how much reality or perfection the idea of the substance affirms of the substance, and how much the idea of the mode affirms of the mode. Since this is so, we also find necessarily that the idea of the substance contains more objective reality than the idea of any accident, and so on. See Proposition 4, Scholium.

V. A thinking thing, if it knows some perfections that it lacks, will immediately attach them to itself, if they are in its power.

Each person observes this in himself, *in as much as he is a thinking being; therefore* (by Proposition 4, Scholium) *we are quite certain of it and for the same reason we are not less certain of the following axiom, namely*:

VI. In the idea or the concept of every thing is contained existence, either possible or necessary (See Descartes' Axiom 10).

Existence is necessary in the concept of God, that is, of the supremely perfect being; for otherwise he would be conceived as an imperfect thing, contrary to the supposed conception: existence contingent or possible in the concept of a limited thing.

VII. Nothing, and no perfection of anything actuall

existing can have nothing, that is, a non-existent thing, as the cause of its existence.

This axiom is as evident to us as I am a thinking being, *as I have shown in Proposition 4, Scholium.*

VIII. Whatever reality or perfection there is in a thing is, either formally or eminently, in its primary and adequate cause.

By eminently *I understand that the cause contains all the reality of the effect more perfectly than the effect itself; by* formally, *that it contains it with equal perfection.*

This axiom depends on the preceding one: for, if it were assumed that there is nothing or less in the cause than in the effect the nothing in the cause would be the cause of the effect. But this is absurd (by the preceding axiom); *therefore no thing whatever can be the cause of some effect, but precisely that thing in which there is eminently, or at least formally, every perfection that is in the effect.*

IX. The objective reality of our ideas requires a cause, in which the same reality is contained, not only objectively, but formally and eminently.

This axiom is accepted by all, although many have misused it. For when anyone conceives anything new, there is no one who does not seek the cause of that concept or idea. When one can assign some cause in which formally or eminently as much reality is contained as there is objectively in that concept, one is satisfied. This is explained by the example of the machine given by Descartes in the Principles, Part I, article 17. So also, if one asks whence man has the ideas of his thinking and of his body, everyone sees that he has them from himself, in as much as he contains formally all that the ideas contain objectively. Therefore, if a man had any idea that contained more objective reality than he himself has formal reality, then, directed by the natural light of reason, we should necessarily seek, outside man himself, another cause that would contain all that perfection formally or eminently. No one has ever assigned a cause other than this one, that he conceived with equal clarity and distinction. Furthermore, in regard to the truth of this axiom, it depends on the preceding. There are (by Axiom 4) *different degrees of reality or entity in the ideas; and accordingly,* (by Axiom 4) *, in proportion to their degree of perfection they require a more perfect cause. But since the degrees of reality,[1] that we observe in the ideas, are not in the ideas in so far as they are considered as modes of thought, but in so far as one represents a substance, and the other only a mode of the substance, or, in a word, in so far as they are considered images of things, it clearly follows that no other first cause of the ideas can be assumed except that which, as we have just shown, all know clearly and distinctly by the natural light of reason, namely, that in which the same reality itself, that they have objectively, is contained formally and eminently. To make it more clearly understood, I shall explain this conclusion by one or two examples. If a person sees books written by one and the same hand* (say one is by a famous philosopher and another by some trifler) *and he pays attention not to the meaning of the words* (that is, in so far as they are images) *, but only to the characters traced and the order of the letters, he will discern no inequality that compels him to seek different causes for the books, but they will seem to have resulted from the same cause and in the same manner.*

But, if he considers the meaning of the words and the contents, he will find a great inequality in the books, and

---

[1] We are also certain of this because we find it in us in so far as we are thinking beings. See the previous Scholium.

will accordingly conclude that the first cause of one book was quite different from the first cause of the other and that one was really more perfect than the other in so far as he found a difference in the meaning of the contents of each book or in the words, in so far as they are considered images.

I now speak of the first cause of the books that must necessarily exist, although I grant and even assume that one book can be copied from another, as is self-evident. Similarly, too, it may be clearly explained by the example of a portrait, let us say of a prince. For if we consider only the material aspect of the portrait, we shall find no inequality between it and other portraits that would force us to seek different causes; nothing in fact will prevent us from thinking that this portrait has been copied from another portrait, and that one in turn from still another, and so on to infinity. For we shall recognize sufficiently that no other cause is required for the delineation of the portrait. But if we regard the picture in so far as it is a picture, we shall immediately be obliged to seek a first cause that contains formally or eminently that which this picture contains representatively. And I do not see anything more to ask in order to establish and clarify this axiom.

X. To conserve a thing, no lesser cause is required than for producing that thing originally.

From the fact that we think at this moment, it does not necessarily follow that we shall think afterward. For the concept that we have of our thought does not involve or contain the necessary existence of thought; for I can clearly and distinctly conceive a thought,[1] although assuming that it does not exist.

---

[1] Each person finds this in himself, in as much as he is a thinking thing.

Now since the nature of every cause must contain in itself or involve the perfection of its own effect (by Axiom 8), *it clearly follows that something in us, or outside us, that we do not yet know, necessarily still exists, the concept or nature of which involves existence, and that is the cause why our thought begins to exist and also that it continues to exist. For, although our thought has begun to exist, its nature and essence do not thereby involve necessary existence more than before its existence and therefore, to continue its existence needs the same power that it needs to begin its existence. And what we say of thought must also be said of every thing whose essence does not involve necessary existence.*

XI. Nothing exists of which it cannot be asked what is the cause (or the reason) for its existence. See Descartes' Axiom 1.

Since existence is something positive, we cannot say that it has nothing as a cause (by Axiom 7): *we must therefore assign some positive cause or reason for a thing's existence, (and that) namely, either an external cause, that is, outside the thing itself, or an internal cause, that is, such as is contained in the nature of the existing thing itself.*

The following four Propositions are taken from Descartes.

PROPOSITION V

The existence of God is known (solely) from a consideration of his nature.

PROOF

To say that something is contained in the nature or concept of a thing is the same as saying that this something itself is true of this thing (*by Definition* 9). But necessary existence is contained in the concept of God (*by Axiom* 6). Therefore it is true to say of God that necessary existence is in him or that he exists.

SCHOLIUM

From this proposition many important results follow; from this fact alone, indeed, that existence belongs to God's nature, or that the concept of God involves necessary existence, as the concept of a triangle that its three angles equal two right angles; or that its existence, no less than its entity, is an eternal truth, almost all the knowledge of God's attributes, that leads us to the love of God or supreme happiness, depends. Therefore it is greatly to be desired that mankind comprehend these matters with us. I admit indeed that certain prejudices exist[1] that prevent each person from understanding them as easily. If however anyone with good intention and impelled only by love of truth and its true use would examine the matter and weigh in his mind what is said in the *Fifth Meditation* and at the end of the *Responses to the First Objections*, and also what we expound about eternity in Part 2, chapter 1 of the *Appendix*, he will unquestionably understand the matter as clearly as possible, and no one will be able to doubt whether he has any idea of God (which is certainly the first basis of human happiness). For he will also see clearly that the idea of God is far different from the ideas of other things; when he understands that God, in so far as regards essences and existence, is completely different from other things. Therefore there is no need to detain the reader any longer on this point.

[1] Read the *Principles*, Part I, article 16.

PROPOSITION VI

The existence of God is proved a posteriori by the fact alone that the idea of him is in us.

PROOF

The objective reality of any of our ideas requires a cause in which this same reality is contained not only objectively but formally or eminently (*by Axiom* 9). Now we have the idea of God (*by Definitions* 2 *and* 8) and the objective reality of this idea is contained in us neither formally nor eminently (*by Axiom* 4) and cannot be contained in anything else but God himself (*by Definition* 8). Hence this idea of God that is in us requires God as a cause, and accordingly God exists (*by Axiom* 7).

SCHOLIUM

There are certain men who deny that they have any idea of God and who still, as they say, worship and love him. And although you set before their eyes the definition and the attributes of God, it will be of no avail; no more in fact than if one tried to teach a man, blind from birth, the distinction of colors as we see them. But, unless we wish to consider them as a new kind of animal, intermediary between man and beast, we ought to have little regard for their words. How, I ask, can we demonstrate the idea of a thing otherwise than by stating its definition and by explaining its attributes? Since we expound this in regard to the idea of God, there is no reason for our lingering over the words of men who deny the idea of God only because they cannot form any image of him in their brain.

It must be observed next that, when Descartes cites Axiom 4 to show that the objective reality of the idea of God is contained neither formally nor eminently in us, he assumes that everyone knows that he is not an infinite substance, that is, supremely knowing, supremely powerful, and so on. He can assume this; for who knows that he thinks also knows that he doubts many things and that he does not know everything clearly and distinctly.

It must be observed finally that according to Definition 8 it also follows clearly that there cannot be several Gods, but one only, as we show clearly in Proposition 11 and in our *Appendix*, Part 2, chapter 2.

PROPOSITION VII

The existence of God is proved also from the fact that we ourselves, who have an idea of him, exist.

SCHOLIUM

To prove this proposition, Descartes assumes these two Axioms, namely:

1. *What can produce what is greater or more difficult can also produce what is smaller.*

2. *It is a greater thing to create or* (by Axiom 10) *to conserve a substance than to create or conserve the attributes or properties of a substance.*

What he means by this I do not know. What does he call easy, or difficult? Nothing is called easy or difficult absolutely[1] but only in respect of its cause. So that one

[1] Not to seek other examples, take the example of a spider that easily spins a web that men could not spin except with the greatest difficulty; on the other hand, men do very easily a very great number of things that are perhaps impossible for angels.

and the same thing, at the same time, in respect of different causes, can be called easy and difficult. But if Descartes calls difficult what can be produced with great labor, and easy what can be produced with less labor by the same cause; as, for example, a force that can raise fifty pounds can raise twenty-five pounds twice as easily; then the axiom will clearly not be absolutely true and he will not be able to prove by it what he proposes. For when he says, *If I had the power to conserve myself, I would also have the power of giving myself all the perfections that are lacking in me* (because they do not require such a great power); I would grant Descartes that the powers that I expend for my conservation could produce many other things far more easily, if I did not need them for my conservation: but, as long as I use them for my conservation, I deny that I can expend them to produce other, though easier, things, as is clearly seen in our example. Nor is the difficulty removed by saying that, being a thinking thing, I ought necessarily to know whether I am expending all my powers for my conservation and also whether that is the cause for my not giving myself the other perfections.

For (apart from the fact that this point is not now under dispute, but only how from this axiom the necessity of this proposition follows) if I knew I would be greater and perhaps I would require, to conserve myself in this greater perfection, greater power than I have, then I do not know if it is a greater task to create a substance than to create (or conserve) attributes; that is, to speak more clearly and more philosophically, I do not know whether a substance does not need all its virtue and essence, by which it perhaps conserves itself, for conserving its attributes.

But let us leave this and let us examine further what

he distinguished author means here; that is, what he understands by easy and difficult. I do not think and I can in no way convince myself that by difficult he understands that which is impossible (and hence no one can conceive in any way how that may be), and by easy that which implies no contradiction (and hence one easily conceives how that may be); although in the *Third Meditation* he seems at first glance to mean this, when he says *I must not believe that things that are lacking in me can perhaps be acquired with more difficulty than those that are already in me. For, on the contrary, it is evident that it was far more difficult for me, that is, a thing or a substance that thinks, to spring from nothing than, and so on.* That would neither be in accordance with the author's words nor would it even suggest his genius. For, to omit the first point, between the possible and the impossible, or between that which is comprehensible and that which is not comprehensible, there is no relationship, just as there is none between something and nothing. A power can no more apply to impossible things than creation and generation to what is non-existent: and on that account no comparison is possible between the possible and the impossible. In addition, I can compare things with each other and find their relationship to each other only when I have a clear and distinct concept of them all. I therefore deny that it follows that he who can do the impossible can also do what is possible. For I ask what kind of reasoning this would be: If a person can square the circle, he can also make a circle in which all the radii that can be drawn from the center to the circumference are equal; or, if anyone can make *nothingness* react and use it as matter from which to produce something, he will likewise have the power to make something out of something?

For, as I have said, between the possible and the impossible and in similar cases, there is no agreement nor analogy, nor comparison, nor any other relationship whatever. And everyone can see this, however slightly he considers the question. I think therefore that this view is altogether at variance with Descartes' genius. But, if I consider the second of the axioms just quoted, it appears that by greater and more difficult he means that which is more perfect, by smaller and easier that which is more imperfect. But this too seems very obscure. For there is the same difficulty here as before: for I deny, as before, that he who can make a thing greater can, at the same time and by the same operation, as must be assumed in the *Proposition*, make what is smaller. Then, when he says that *it is a greater thing to create (or conserve) a substance than attributes,* he surely cannot mean by attributes that which is formally contained in the substance and is distinguished from the substance itself only by Reason.

For then to create a substance is the same thing as to create attributes. Nor, by the same reasoning, can he mean the properties of the substance that necessarily follow from its essence and definition. Still less can he mean, although he seems to do so, the properties and the attributes of another substance; as, for example, if I say that I have the power to conserve myself, a finite thinking substance, I cannot on that account say that I have also the power of giving myself the perfections of the infinite substance, that differs in all its essence from mine. For the force or the essence by which I conserve[1] myself in

[1] Note that the force by which a substance is conserved is nothing outside its essence and differs from it only in name; this question will have its place especially when we treat the power of God, in the Appendix.

my being is completely different from the force or essence by which an absolutely infinite substance conserves itself, from which its strength and properties are distinguished only by Reason. And so (although I were to suppose that I conserved myself), if I wanted to conceive that I can give myself the perfections of the absolutely infinite substance, I would be merely supposing that I could reduce to nothing all my essence and then create an infinite substance. That would certainly be far greater than to suppose only that I could conserve myself as a finite substance.

And so, since by attributes or properties he can mean none of these things, nothing else could be meant but the qualities that the substance itself eminently contains (as such and such a thought in the mind, that I clearly perceive to be lacking in me), not those that another substance eminently contains (as such and such a motion in extension: for such perfections are not perfections to me, as a thinking being, and so are not lacking in me). But then what Descartes wants to prove can in no wise be concluded from this axiom: namely, that, if I conserve myself, I also have the power of giving myself all the perfections that I clearly find belonging to the supremely perfect being, as is clearly established by what has been said. But, not to leave the matter unproved and to avoid all confusion, it seemed best to prove first the following Lemmata and then to build upon them the proof of Proposition 7.

LEMMA I

The more perfect a thing is by its own nature, the greater and more necessary is the existence that it involves; and inversely, the more necessary the existence that a thing involves by its own nature, the more perfect it is.

PROOF

In the idea or concept of everything is contained existence (*by Axiom* 6). Let A then be a thing assumed to have ten degrees of perfection. I say that its concept involves more existence than if it were assumed to contain only five degrees of perfection. For since we can affirm no existence of nothingness (*See Scholium of Proposition* 4), whatever we take away from A's perfection by thought and accordingly more and more conceive it as participating in nothingness, so much possibility of existence too do we deny it. And hence, if we conceive the degrees of its perfection diminished to infinity, to zero or a cipher, A will contain no existence or an absolutely impossible existence. If, on the contrary, we increase its degrees to infinity, we shall conceive it as involving supreme existence, and hence supremely necessary. This is the first part. Then, since necessity and perfection can in no sense be separated (*as is sufficiently established from Axiom* 6 *and the entire first part of this Proof*); it clearly follows what was proposed for proof in the second place.

Observation 1: Although many things are said to exist necessarily from the fact alone that a determined cause exists to produce them, it is not of these things that we shall speak here, but only of that necessity and possibility that follow from the sole consideration of the nature or the essence of a thing, without regard to any cause.

Observation 2: We are not speaking here of beauty and the other perfections that men have wanted to call perfections through superstition and ignorance. But I understand by perfection only reality or being; as, for example, I perceive that more reality is contained in the substance than in the modes or accidents; and consequently I know clearly that it contains more necessary and more perfect existence than the accidents, as is sufficiently established from Axioms 4 and 6.

COROLLARY

It follows hence that whatever involves necessary existence is a being supremely perfect, that is, God.

LEMMA II

Whoever has the power to conserve himself, has a nature involving necessary existence.

PROOF

Whoever has the power of self-conservation also has the power of self-creation (*by Axiom* 10), that is (as all will readily grant), needs no external cause in order to exist, his nature alone being a sufficient cause for his existence, either possibly or necessarily. But not possibly; for (*by what I have proved about Axiom* 10) then it would not follow that, from the fact that he already existed, he would exist afterward (which is contrary to the hypothesis). Therefore, necessarily; that is, his nature involves necessary existence.   Q.E.D.

PROOF of Proposition VII

If I had the power of self-conservation, I would have such a nature that I would involve necessary existence *(by Lemma* 2); therefore *(by the Corollary of Lemma* 1) my nature would contain all the perfections. But I find in me, in as much as I am a thinking thing, many imperfections, as doubting, desiring, and so on of which I am certain *(by the Scholium of Proposition* 4); therefore I have no power of self-conservation. Nor can I say that I now lack these perfections because I now want to deny myself of them; for that would clearly refute the first Lemma and what I find clearly in myself *(by Axiom* 5).

Next I cannot exist now without being conserved, so long as I exist, either by myself, if I have such power, or by another who has that power *(by Axioms* 10 and 11). But I exist *(by the Scholium of Proposition* 4), and yet I do not have the power of self-conservation, as has just been proved; therefore I am conserved by another. But not by another who does not have the power of self-conservation (for the same reason by which I have just shown that I am myself incapable of self-conservation); therefore, by another who has the power of self-conservation, that is *(by Lemma* 2), whose nature involves necessary existence, that is *(by the Corollary of Lemma* 1), who contains all the perfections which I clearly know belong to the being supremely perfect, that is *(by Definition* 8), God, exists.   Q.E.D.

COROLLARY

God can create all the things that we clearly perceive, according as we perceive them.

PROOF

All these things follow clearly from the preceding Proposition. For in it the existence of God is proved

40

from the fact that someone must exist in whom there are all the perfections of which some idea is in us. Now there is in us the idea of some power so great that by him alone, in whom this power resides, heaven, earth, and also all other things that are comprehended by me as possible, can be created. Therefore along with the existence of God all these things as well have been proved by him.

PROPOSITION VIII

The mind and the body are really distinct.

PROOF

Whatever we perceive clearly, that can be created by God in the manner we perceive it (*by the preceding corollary*). But we clearly perceive the mind, that is (*by Definition* 6), a thinking substance, without body (*by Definition* 7), without any extended substance (*by Propositions 3 and* 4) and, inversely, the body without mind (as all readily agree). Therefore, at least by the divine power, the mind can exist without the body and the body without the mind.

Furthermore, the substances that can be one without the other are really distinct (*by Definition* 10); now the mind and the body are substances (*by Definitions* 5, 6, 7) that can exist one without the other (*as has just been proved*); therefore the mind and the body are really distinct.

See Proposition 4 at the end of Descartes' *Responses to the Second Objections*; and Part I of the *Principles* from article 22 to article 29. For I do not consider it knowing.   Q.E.D.

SCHOLIUM

If this is denied, then God either knows nothing, or not everything, or only certain things. But to know certain things only and not to know other things assumes a limited and imperfect understanding, which it is absurd to ascribe to God (*by Definition* 8). As for God knowing nothing, that indicates either a lack of understanding in God, as in the case of men who know nothing, and it involves imperfection that cannot happen to God (*by the same Definition*); or it indicates that for him to know anything is contrary to the perfection of God. But, since understanding is altogether denied to him, he will not be able to create any understanding (*by Axiom* 8). Now, since understanding is clearly and distinctly perceived by us, God can be the cause of this (*by the Corollary to Proposition* 7). Therefore for him to know something is far from being contrary to the perfection of God. Therefore he will be supremely worth while to transcribe them here.

PROPOSITION IX

God is supremely knowing.

PROOF

Although it must be granted that God is incorporeal, as is proved by Proposition 16, this however must not be considered as if all the perfections of extensions should be withdrawn from him, but only in so far as the nature of the extension and the properties involve some imperfection. The same statement also must be made about the intelligence of God, as all admit who want to acquire wisdom beyond the crowd of philosophers, as will be explained at length in our Appendix, Part 2, chapter 7.

PROPOSITION X

Whatever perfection is found in God comes from God.

PROOF

If it is denied, let it be assumed that there is in God some perfection that is not from God. This perfection will be in God, or by itself, or by some being different from God. If it is by itself, it will then have necessary existence or at least possible existence (*by Lemma 2, Proposition 7*) and so it will be something supremely perfect (*by Corollary, Lemma 1 of the same Proposition*), and hence (*by Definition 8*) God. If then it is said that there is something in God that is by itself, it is like saying that it is from God. Q.E.D.

If however it is in God from a being different from God, God cannot be conceived as supremely perfect by himself, which is contrary to Definition 8. Therefore whatever perfection is found in God is from God.

Q.E.D.

PROPOSITION XI

Several Gods cannot exist.

PROOF

If it is denied, conceive, if it is possible, several Gods, for example, A and B. Then necessarily (*by Proposition*

9) both A and B will be supremely intelligent, that is, A will know everything, that is, it will know itself and B, and inversely B will know itself and A. But, since A and B exist necessarily (*by Proposition* 5), the cause of truth and of the necessity of the idea of B, which is in A, is B itself; and, on the other hand, the cause of truth and of the necessity of the idea of A, which is in B, is A itself. Therefore there will be some perfection in A that is not from A, and in B some perfection that is not from B; and hence (*by the preceding Proposition*) neither A nor B will be Gods; and so there cannot be several Gods.   Q.E.D.

It must here be observed that from this fact alone, that some thing involves from itself necessary existence, as God, it necessarily follows that it is unique; as every one will be able to recognize by deep meditation within himself, and as I could have shown here, but not in a manner as perceptible to all as was done in this Proposition.

PROPOSITION XII

All that exists is conserved by the power of God alone.

PROOF

If it is denied, let it be assumed that something conserves itself; therefore (*by Lemma* 2, *Proposition* 7) its nature involves necessary existence; and hence (*by the Corollary of Lemma* 1 *of Proposition* 7) it would be God, and there would be several Gods, which is absurd (*by the preceding Proposition*). Therefore nothing exists that is not conserved by the power of God alone.

Q.E.D.

COROLLARY I

God is the Creator of all things.

PROOF

God (*by the preceding Proposition*) conserves, that is (*by Axiom* 10), all that exists he created and still continues to create.

COROLLARY II

A thing has no essence in itself that is the cause of cognition of God; but on the contrary God is the cause of things in relation also to their essence.

PROOF

Since no perfection is found in God that is not from God (*by Proposition* 10), things will have no essence in themselves that can be the cause of cognition of God. But on the contrary, since God has created nothing from another thing but has created directly (*by Proposition* 12 *and Corollary*) and the act of creation recognizes no other cause except the efficient cause (for that is how I define creation) which is God, it follows that things before creation were absolutely nothing and accordingly that God too was the cause of their essence.

Q.E.D.

It should be noted that this Corollary is also evident from the fact that God is the cause or creator of all things (*by Corollary* 1) and that the cause must contain in itself all the perfections of the effect (*by Axiom* 8), as everyone can easily perceive.

COROLLARY III

Hence it follows clearly that God does not feel and properly speaking does not perceive; for his understanding is not determined by anything outside himself, but everything flows from him

COROLLARY IV

God is by his causality anterior to the essence and existence of things, as clearly follows from Corollaries 1 and 2 of the preceding Proposition.

PROPOSITION XIII

God is supremely veracious and in no sense deceptive.

PROOF

We can imaginatively attribute to God nothing (*by Definition* 8) in which we recognize any imperfection. And since all deceit (as is self-evident[1]) or the will to deceive originates solely from malice or fear—fear assuming a diminution of power and malice a deprivation of goodness—no deceit or will to deceive can be attributed to God, that is, to a being supremely powerful

---

[1] I have not listed this axiom among the axioms, because there was no need to do so. I did not require it, except to prove this proposition only, and also because, as long as I did not know the existence of God, I was unwilling to accept the truth of anything except what I could deduce from the first thing known: *I am*, as I have indicated in the Scholium, Proposition 4. Furthermore, I did not list the definitions of fear and malice among the definitions, because no one is unaware of them, and I did not require them except for this proposition alone.

and supremely good, but on the contrary he must be considered supremely veracious and in no sense deceitful.

Q.E.D.

See the *Response* to the *Second Objections,* number 4.

PROPOSITION XIV

Whatever we perceive clearly and distinctly is true.

PROOF

The faculty of distinguishing between truth and falsehood which is in us (as everyone discovers in himself and as it is possible to see from all that has already been proved) was created by God and is continuously conserved by him (*by Proposition* 12 *and Corollaries*); that is (*by the preceding Proposition*), by a being supremely veracious and in no sense whatever deceitful; and he has not given us any power (as everyone discovers in himself) of withholding belief in those things that we perceive clearly and distinctly, or of not assenting to them. Therefore, if we were deceived in regard to them, we would be completely deceived by God and he would be deceitful, which is absurd (*by the preceding Proposition*).

Whatever therefore we perceive clearly and distinctly is true.

Q.E.D.

SCHOLIUM

Since those things to which we necessarily assent when they are perceived by us clearly and distinctly are necessarily true; and since we have the faculty (as everyone discovers in himself) of not assenting to those things that are obscure and doubtful, that is, those things that are not deduced from the most convincing principles; it clearly follows that we can always take care not to fall into error and never to be deceived (this will be understood still more clearly from what follows); provided we seriously decide for ourselves to affirm nothing that we do not perceive clearly and distinctly, that is, that has not been deduced from clear and certain principles.

PROPOSITION XV

Error is not something positive.

PROOF

If error were something positive, it would have only God as a cause, by whom it would have to be created continuously (*by Proposition* 12). But that is absurd (*by Proposition* 13). Therefore error is not something positive.   Q.E.D.

SCHOLIUM

Since error is not something positive in man, it cannot be anything else but the negation of the proper use of freedom (*by the Scholium of Proposition* 14); and so only in the sense in which we say that the absence of the sun is the cause of darkness, or in which God is said to be the cause of blindness, because he created a child like others except for sight, can God be said to be the cause of error: because he has given us an understanding that extends only to a few things. To understand this clearly, and at the same time how error comes solely from the abuse of our will, and finally how we can avoid error; let us recall to our memory all the modes of thought that we have, that is, all the modes of perceiving (as feeling, imagining, and purely knowing) and of wishing (as desiring, shunning, affirming, denying, and doubting); for all of them can be reduced to these two.

In regard to them it must now be noted: 1), that the mind, in so far as it understands things clearly and distinctly, and gives assent to them, cannot be deceived (*by Proposition* 14): not in so far as it only perceives things without giving its assent to them. For, although I should now perceive a winged horse, it is certain that this perception contains nothing false as long as I do not assent that it is true that a winged horse exists and even as long as I doubt whether a winged horse exists. And since to assent is merely to determine one's will, it follows that error depends solely on the use of the will.

To clarify this still further, it must be noted: 2), that we have the power not only of giving assent to those things that we perceive clearly and distinctly, but also to those things that we perceive in any other manner whatever.

For our will is not determined by any limits. This everyone can see clearly, provided he considers that, if God wanted to make our faculty of understanding infinite, he would not require to give us a greater faculty of assent than the faculty that we now have for us to be able to assent to everything understood by us. But this same faculty, that we now have, would suffice for affirming an infinite number of things. And we also experience really that we assent to many things that we have not deduced from established principles. Furthermore, it is clearly evident from this that, if the understanding extended as far as the faculty of the will, or if the faculty of the will could not extend beyond the understanding, or if, lastly, we could restrain the faculty of the will within the limits of the under-standing, we should never fall into error (*by Proposition* 14).

But we have no power to make the understanding extend as far as the faculty of the will, or the will not extend beyond the understanding: for that implies that the will is not infinite and that the understanding is not created finite. It remains therefore to consider the third question: whether we have the power to contain our faculty of the will within the limits of the understanding. Now since the will is free to determine itself, it follows that we have the power of containing the faculty of assent within the limits of the understanding and hence of avoiding falling into error; hence it is very clearly evident that our never being deceived depends solely on the use of the freedom of the will. That our will is free is proved in Article 39, Part I of the *Principles* and in the *Fourth Meditation,* and by us too in great detail in our *Appendix,* last chapter. And, although, when we perceive a thing clearly and distinctly, we cannot refuse assent to it, that necessary assent does not depend on the weakness, but solely on the freedom and perfection of our will.

For to assent is in us perfection (as is sufficiently well known by itself) nor is the will ever more perfect or more free than when it is entirely self-determining. As this can occur when the mind understands something clearly and distinctly, of necessity it will at once assume that perfection for itself (*by Axiom* 5). Therefore it is far from being the case that, when we are least indiffer-ent in comprehending the truth, we should consider ourselves as less free. For on the contrary we hold it certain that, the more we are indifferent, the less free we are.

It only remains therefore to explain here how error in respect to man is nothing but privation, and in respect to God mere negation. We shall see this easily, if we observe first that, from the fact that we perceive many things apart from those that we clearly understand, we are more perfect than if we did not perceive them: as is quite evident from the fact that, if it were assumed that we could perceive nothing clearly and distinctly, but only confusedly, we should have no greater perfection than the confused perception of things and no other thing would be desired for our nature. Further, to assent to things, however confused, is perfection, in so far as it is an act. This will be clear to everyone if, as before, it is assumed that clear and distinct perception is contrary to man's nature; for then it will be evident that it is far better for man to assent to things though confused and to exercise freedom than to remain always indifferent, that is (as we have just shown) in the lowest degree of freedom. And if we also consider the use and the interest of human life, we shall find it absolutely necessary, and daily experience is a good teacher for everyone.

Since therefore all the modes of thought that we have, in so far as they are considered in themselves alone, are perfect, that which constitutes the form of error cannot exist in them as such. But if we consider the modes of the will, in so far as they differ from each other, we shall find some more perfect than others, in so far as some make the will less indifferent, that is, more free, than others. Then we shall also see that, as long as we assent to confused things, we make the mind less apt to distinguish true and false, and accordingly we lack freedom in the best sense. Therefore to assent to confused things, in so far as that is something positive, contains no imperfection or form of error; but only in so far as we thus deprive ourselves of the best form of freedom that belongs to our nature and is in our power. All the imperfection of error then will consist solely of the privation of the best form of freedom; this is called error. It is called privation because we are deprived of some perfection demanded by our nature. Error, because we lack this perfection through our own fault, in as much as we do not contain the will, as far as we can, within the limits of the understanding.

Since therefore error is nothing, in respect to man, but the privation of the perfect or right use of freedom, it follows that it does not reside in any faculty that it has from God, nor in any operation of the faculties in so far as it depends on God. Nor can we say that God has deprived us of a greater understanding than he could have given us and hence made us capable of falling into error. For the nature of no thing can demand anything of God nor does anything belong to anything apart from that which the will of God has wished to bestow on it; for nothing exists and can even be conceived before the will of God; (as is fully explained in our Appendix, chapters 7 and 8). Therefore God has not deprived us of greater understanding, or of a more perfect faculty of understanding, any more than he has deprived the circle of the properties of the sphere, or the circumference of the properties of the sphere.

Since therefore none of our faculties, however considered, can show any imperfection in God, it clearly follows that the imperfection of which the form of error consists is only, in respect to man, a privation: but related to God, as to its cause, it cannot be called a privation, but only a negation.

PROPOSITION XVI

God is incorporeal.

PROOF

The body is the immediate subject of spatial motion *(by Definition* 7); therefore, if God were corporeal, he would be divided into parts: since this clearly involves an imperfection, it is absurd to affirm it of God *(by Definition* 8).

ANOTHER PROOF

If God were corporeal, he could be divided into parts *(by Definition* 7). Now each part could either subsist by itself, or could not so subsist: if it could not, it would be like the other things that have been created by God, and hence, like everything created, it would be continuously created by God by the same power *(by Proposition* 10 *and Axiom* 11), and would not belong to God's nature any more than the other created things, which is absurd *(by Proposition* 5). But if each part subsists by itself, each part must also involve necessary existence *(by Lemma* 2 *of Proposition* 7), and consequently each part would be a supremely perfect being *(by Corollary to Lemma* 2, *Proposition* 7). But this too is absurd *(by Proposition* 11): therefore God is incorporeal.

Q.E.D.

PROPOSITION XVII

God is a very simple being.

PROOF

If God were composed of parts, these parts would have to be, at least by their nature, anterior to God (as all will readily admit), which is absurd (*by Corollary 4 of Proposition* 12). Therefore he is a very simple being.

Q.E.D.

COROLLARY

It follows from this that the intelligence of God, his will, or his Decree and his Power are not distinct from his essence except in our thinking.

PROPOSITION XVIII

God is immutable.

PROOF

If God were changeable, he could not change partially but would have to change according to his entire essence (*by Proposition* 7). But the essence of God exists necessarily (*by Propositions* 5, 6, *and* 7); therefore God is immutable.

Q.E.D.

PROPOSITION XIX

God is eternal.

PROOF

God is a being supremely perfect (*by Definition* 8) hence it follows (*by Proposition* 5) that he exists necessarily. Now if we attribute to him a limited existence the limits of that existence must necessarily be known if not to us, at least to God himself *(by Proposition* 9), because he is supremely intelligent; therefore God will know himself beyond those limits, that is *(by Definition* 8, will know a supremely perfect being as non-existent, which is absurd *(by Proposition* 5). Therefore God has an infinite, not a limited existence, that we call eternity. (See chapter 1, Part 2 of our Appendix.) Therefore God is eternal.   Q.E.D

PROPOSITION XX

God has preordained everything from eternity.

PROOF

Since God is eternal *(by the preceding Proposition),* his intelligence is eternal, because it belongs to his eternal essence *(by the Corollary to Proposition* 17). But his understanding does not differ in fact from his will or decree *(by the Corollary to Proposition* 17); therefore, when we say that God has known things from eternity, we are likewise saying that he has thus willed or decreed things from eternity.   Q.E.D.

COROLLARY

From this Proposition it follows that God is supremely consistent in his operations.

PROPOSITION XXI

A substance extended in length, width, and depth really exists; and we are united to one of its parts.

PROOF

An extended thing, according to our clear and distinct perception of it, does not belong to the Nature of God (*by Proposition* 10). But it can be created by God (*by Corollary to Proposition* 7 *and by Proposition* 8). Now we perceive clearly and distinctly (as everyone discovers in himself, in so far as he thinks) that the extended substance is a cause sufficient to produce in us pleasure, grief, and similar ideas or sensations that are continuously produced in us against our will. But, if we want to imagine a cause of our sensations other than the extended substance, say God or an Angel, we at once destroy the clear and distinct concept that we have. Therefore,[1] as long as we pay strict attention to our perceptions without admitting anything, except what is perceived clearly and distinctly, we shall be quite inclined, or least indifferent, to the affirmation that the extended substance is the sole cause of our sensations; and accordingly to the affirmation that an extended thing created by God exists. And in this respect we cannot be deceived (*by Proposition* 14, *with Scholium*). Therefore it is truthfully affirmed that a substance extended in length, width, and depth exists: which was the first point to prove.

Further, we observe a great difference among our sensations, which (as we have just proved) must be produced in us from an extended substance; as when we say that I feel or I see a tree, or when I say I am thirsty or that I suffer, and so on. Now I see that I cannot perceive clearly the cause of the difference, unless I first know that I am closely united to one part of matter and not likewise to the other parts. Since I know this

[1] See the proof of Proposition 14, and Proposition 15, Scholium.

clearly and distinctly, and that this cannot be perceived by me in any other way, it is true (*by Proposition* 14, *with Scholium*) that I am united to one part of matter. This was the second point. We have therefore proved it.

Q.E.D

Note: Unless the reader here considers himself only as a thinking being, without body, and rejects as preconceptions all the reasons that he had previously had for believing that the body exists, his attempt to understand this proof will be useless.

PART II

POSTULATE

Here it is asked only that everyone consider his perceptions with the greatest possible care in order to be able to distinguish what is clear and obscure.

DEFINITIONS

I. *Extension* is that which consists of three dimensions; but we do not understand by extension the act of extending or anything different from quantity.

II. By *Substance* we understand that which needs, in order to exist, only the co-operation of God.

III. An *Atom* is a part of matter indivisible by its nature.

IV. *Indefinite* is that whose limits (if it has any) cannot be investigated by human understanding.

V. *Void* is extension without corporeal substance.

VI. Between *Space* and extension we make no distinction except in our thinking, that is, there is no real difference. Read Article 10, Part 2 of the *Principles*.

VII. That which we know can be divided mentally, that is, is *divisible*, at least potentially.

VIII. *Spatial Motion* is a transference of one part of matter, or of a body, from the vicinity of those bodies that touch it immediately and are considered as motionless, to the vicinity of other bodies.

Descartes uses this definition to explain spatial motion. To understand it properly, it must be considered:

1. *That by a part of matter he understands all that is transferred at the same time, although that itself may in turn be composed of many parts.*

2. *That, to avoid confusion in this definition, he speaks only of that which is always in the movable thing, that is, transference, which is not to be confused, as has occasionally been done by others, with the force or the action that transfers. It is commonly thought that this force or action is required for motion only, not for rest: this is a total misconception. For, as is self-evident, the same force is required for certain degrees of motion to be exerted at the same time on any body in respose as for those certain degrees of motion to be withdrawn in turn from the same body, so that it comes to rest. This is even proved by experience: for we use almost the same force to move a ship at rest in stagnant water as to halt it suddenly when it moves; and certainly the force would be the same if we were not helped in holding back the ship by the weight and inertia of the water displaced by the ship.*

3. *That he says that transference occurs from the vicinity of contiguous bodies to the vicinity of other bodies, but not from one place to another. For a place (as he himself has explained in Article 13, Part 2) is not something real but depends only on our thought, so that the same body may be said to change place and yet not to change; but not that it is transferred from the vicinity of a contiguous body and at the same time not transferred; for only certain bodies can at the same moment be contiguous to the same mobile body.*

4. That he does not say that transference can occur absolutely from the vicinity of contiguous bodies, but only of those that are considered as being at rest. For, to transfer a body A from a body B at rest, the same force and action are required from one direction as from the other; this is quite apparent from the example of a boat clinging to the mud or the sand at the bottom of the water; for in order to dislodge it, equal force will necessarily have to be applied to the bottom of the water as to the boat. Therefore the force, by which the bodies

must be moved, is exerted equally on the moving body and on the body at rest. Transference therefore is reciprocal; for, if the boat is removed from the sand, the sand too is removed from the boat. So, if, in an absolute sense, we wanted to attribute equal motions in different directions to one and the other of two bodies that are separated from each other and to consider one of them not at rest, and that only because there is the same action in one as in the other; then we should be forced to attribute just as much motion to the bodies considered by all as at rest, for example, to the sand from which the boat is separated, as to the moving bodies; for, as we have shown, the same action is required from one direction as from the other, and the transference is reciprocal. But this would be too much at variance with the common manner of speaking. However, although those bodies, from which others are separated, are considered at rest, and are even so called, yet we shall recall that all that is in a moving body, on account of which it is said to move, is also in the body at rest.

5. *Finally, it also appears clearly from the Definition that every body has only one motion peculiar to itself, since it is understood to withdraw from certain bodies only that are contiguous to it and motionless. However, if the moving body is a part of other bodies, having other motions, we know clearly that it can also participate in numberless other motions; but, as so many motions cannot easily be conceived at the same time and cannot even all be recognized, it will be sufficient to consider in each body only the motion that is peculiar to that body.*

Read Article 31, Part 2 of the *Principles*.

IX. By a *Circle of Moving Bodies* we understand only what occurs, when the last body, moving by the impulsion of another body, immediately touches the first of the moving bodies; although the line described by all the bodies by the impulsion of one motion at the same time is very distorted.

AXIOMS

I. Nothingness has no properties.

II. Whatever can be taken away from something, without affecting its integrity, does not constitute its essence; but that which, if it is taken away, destroys the thing, constitutes its essence.

III. In hardness, sense tells us nothing else, nor do we know anything else about it clearly and distinctly, except that the parts of hard bodies resist the motion of our hands.

IV. If two bodies approach each other, or recede from

each other, they will not on that account occupy a larger or smaller space.

V. A part of matter, whether it yields or resists, does not on that account lose the nature of its body.

VI. Motion, rest, shape, and similar ideas cannot be conceived without extension.

VII. Apart from the sensory qualities nothing remains in a body except extension and its affections, mentioned in Part I of the *Principles*.

VIII. A space, or an extension, cannot be greater at one time than at another.

IX. Every extension can be divided, at least in thought.

No one who has learned the elements of mathematics can doubt the truth of this Axiom. For the given space between the tangent and the circle can always be divided by an infinite number of other greater circles. The same thing is also evident from the asymptotes of a hyperbole.

X. No one can conceive the limits of any extension or space unless he also conceives beyond these limits themselves other spaces immediately following the first space.

XI. If matter is multiple and one matter does not immediately touch another, each is necessarily composed under the limits beyond which matter does not exist.

XII. The most minute bodies yield easily to the motion of our hands.

XIII. A space does not penetrate another space, and is not greater at one time more than at another time.

XIV. If pipe A is of the same length as C and C twice as large as A, and if some fluid passes twice as quickly through pipe A as that which passes through pipe C, as much matter will pass through pipe A in the same space of time as through pipe C. And if as much matter passes through pipe A as through C, the matter passing through pipe A will move twice as quickly.

XV. Things that agree with a third, agree with each other. And things that are double the same third are equal to each other.

XVI. Matter that moves in different ways has at least as many parts actually divided as the various degrees of speed that are observed at the same time in the matter.

XVII. The shortest line between two points is a straight line.

XVIII. The body A that moves from C to B, if repelled by a contrary impulsion, will move through the same line toward C.

XIX. Bodies that have contrary motions, when they meet together, are both forced to experience some change, or at least one of the two bodies.

XX. Change in a thing proceeds from a greater force.

XXI. If, when body 1 moves toward body 2, and im-

pels it, and body 8 moves by this impulsion toward 1, bodies 1, 2, 3, etc. cannot be in a straight line: but all, including 1, form a complete circle: see Definition 9.

LEMMA I

Where there is Extension or Space, a Substance is necessarily there.

PROOF

Extension or space (*by Axiom* 1) cannot be absolute nothingness; it is therefore an attribute, which must necessarily be assigned to something. Not to God (*by Proposition* 16, *Part* I): then to a thing that, in order to exist, needs only the co-operation of God (*by Proposition* 12, *Part* I), that is, to a substance (*by Definition* 2 of *Part* II). Q.E.D.

LEMMA II

Rarefaction and Condensation are conceived clearly and distinctly by us although we do not admit that bodies occupy in rarefaction more space than in condensation.

PROOF

They can be conceived clearly and distinctly by the mere fact that the parts of any body withdraw from each other and approach each other. Therefore (*by Axiom* 4) they will occupy neither a larger nor a smaller space. For, if the parts of a body, say a sponge, from the mere fact that they approach each other, expel the bodies with which the intervals are filled; by that very fact alone this body will become more dense, but its parts will not on that account occupy less space than before (*by Axiom* 4). And if they again withdraw from each other, and the interstices are filled by other bodies, arefaction will take place, yet the parts will not occupy greater space. And what, with the aid of the senses we early perceive in the sponge, we can perceive by the nderstanding alone for all bodies, although the intervals of the parts elude entirely the human sense. Therefore Rarefaction and Condensation are clearly nd distinctly conceived by us, and so on.

Q.E.D.

It seemed fitting to preface here the above remarks so s to clarify the understanding of its preconceptions of pace, rarefaction, and so on, and to make it fit to undertand what follows.

PROPOSITION I

Although hardness, weight, and other sensory qualities re taken away from a body, the nature of the body will evertheless remain unaffected.

PROOF

In the case of hardness, say of a stone, sense tells us othing more, nor do we know clearly and distinctly nything more than that the parts of hard bodies resist he motion of our hands (*by Axiom* 3). Therefore (*by Proposition* 14, *Part* I) hardness too will be nothing else. f the body is reduced to as minute particles of powder s possible, its parts will yield (*by Axiom* 12) easily and et will not lose the nature of the body (*by Axiom* 5).

Q.E.D.

In regard to weight and other sensory qualities, the roof proceeds in the same manner.

PROPOSITION II

The nature of a body or matter consists solely of ex tension.

PROOF

The nature of a body is not destroyed by the with drawal of the sensory qualities (*by Proposition* I, *Par* II); therefore they do not constitute its essence (*by Axiom* 2). Therefore nothing remains except extension and its affections (*by Axiom* 7). Therefore, if extension is withdrawn, nothing will be left that belongs to the nature of the body, but it will be completely destroyed therefore (*by Axiom* 2) the nature of the body consist solely of extension.   Q.E.D

COROLLARY

Space and body are not really different.

PROOF

Body and extension are not really different (*by the preceding Proposition*); space also and extension are not really different (*by Definition* 6); therefore (*by Axiom* 15) space and body are not really different.

Q.E.D.

SCHOLIUM

Although we say[1] that God is ubiquitous, it is not admitted on that account that God is extended, that i

[1] See on these points more explicit details in the *Appendix*, *Par* II, chapter 3 and 9.

(*by the preceding Proposition*), corporeal; for his ubiquity refers solely to the power of God and his co-operation by means of which he conserves all things; so that the ubiquity of God refers not to extension or body any more than to angels or human souls. But it must be observed that, when we say that his power is ubiquitous, we do not exclude his essence; for, wherever his power is, there also is his essence (*Corollary to Proposition 17, Part* I); but only that we exclude his corporeality, that is, that God is not ubiquitous by some corporeal power, but by a divine power or essence, that equally conserves extension and thinking things (*Proposition 17, Part* I); this he certainly could not have conserved, if his power, that is, his essence, were corporeal.

PROPOSITION III

It is a contradiction for a void to exist.

PROOF

By void is understood extension without corporeal substance (*by Definition* 5), that is (*by Proposition* 2, *Part* II), a body without a body, which is absurd.

For a fuller explanation and for correcting a preconception about void, read Articles 17 and 18, Part II *of the Principles, where it is specially noted that bodies between which nothing is interposed necessarily touch each other and also that nothingness has no properties.*

PROPOSITION IV

The same part of a body does not occupy more space at one time than at another time and inversely the same space does not contain more body at one time than at another.

PROOF

Space and body are not really different (*by Corollary to Proposition 2, Part* II). Therefore, when we say that a space is not greater at one time than at another (*by Axiom* 13), we are also saying that a body cannot be greater, that is, occupy more space, at one time than at another. This was the first point. Further, from the fact that space and body do not really differ, it follows that, when we say that a body cannot occupy a greater space at one time than at another, we are simply saying that the same space cannot contain more body at one time than at another. Q.E.D.

COROLLARY

Bodies that occupy the same space, say gold and air, have an equal amount of matter or corporeal substance.

PROOF

A corporeal substance consists not of hardness, for example gold, nor of softness, for example air, nor of any of the sensory qualities (*by Proposition* I, *Part* II), but solely of extension (*by Proposition* II, *Part* II). Now since (*by hypothesis*) there is as much space, that is, extension, in the one as in the other, there is therefore as much corporeal substance. Q.E.D.

PROPOSITION V

Atoms do not exist.

PROOF

Atoms are parts of matter indivisible by their nature (*by Definition* 3). But, since the nature of matter consists of extension (*by Proposition* 2, *Part* II) which, however small, is divisible by its nature (*by Axiom* 9 *and Definition* 7), a part of matter, however small, is therefore divisible by its nature; that is, there are no Atoms or parts of matter indivisible by their nature.

Q.E.D.

SCHOLIUM

The questions of Atoms has always been important and complicated. Some affirm the existence of Atoms from the fact that an infinity cannot be greater than another infinity: and, if two quantities, say A and a quantity double the amount of A, are divisible to infinity, they will also, by the power of God who knows their infinite parts at a glance, be able to be actually divided into infinite parts. Therefore, since, as has been said, one infinity cannot be greater than another infinity, the quantity A will be equal to double the quantity of A, which is absurd. They also ask whether half of an infinite number is also infinite; and whether it is equal or unequal, and other questions of a like tenor. To all this Descartes replies that we ought not to reject those things that come within our understanding and are accordingly perceived clearly and distinctly, on account of other things that pass our understanding or comprehension and hence are perceived by us only very inadequately. Now infinity and its properties transcend human understanding, which is finite by nature; and so it would be inept to reject as false what we conceive clearly and distinctly about space, or to doubt it because of our inability to comprehend infinity. And for this reason Descartes considers infinite the things in which we observe no limits, such as the extension of the universe, the divisibility of the parts of matter, and so forth. Read Article 26, Part I of the *Principles*.

PROPOSITION VI

Matter is indefinitely extended, and the matter of heaven and of earth is one and the same.

PROOF

1. *Proof of the first part.*

We can imagine no limits to extension, that is (*by Proposition* 2, *Part* II), to matter, without conceiving beyond these limits themselves other spaces following immediately (*by Axiom* 10), that is (*by Definition* 6), extension or matter, and that to infinity. This was the first point.

2. *Proof of the second part.*

The essence of matter consists of extension (*by Proposition* 2, *Part* II) and it is infinite (*by the first part of this proof*), that is (*by Definition* 4), it cannot be perceived under any limits by human understanding: therefore (*by Axiom* 11) it is not multiple, but everywhere one and the same. This was the second point.

SCHOLIUM

Up to this point we have discussed the nature or essence of extension. That it exists, created by God, such as we conceive it, we have proved in the last Proposition of Part I; and from Proposition 12, Part I it follows that it is now conserved by the same power that created it. Further, in the same last Proposition, Part I, we have proved that we, in so far as thinking things, are united to some part of that matter by whose aid we perceived that all those variations actually exist of which, from the mere contemplation of matter, we know it is capable: as divisibility, spatial motion, or the movement of one part from one place to another, that we perceive clearly and distinctly, provided that we know that other parts of matter take the place of the transferred parts. And this division and this motion are conceived by us in an infinite number of ways, and hence infinite variations too of matter are conceived by us. I say that they are clearly and distinctly conceived by us, as long as we conceive them as modes of extension, not as things really distinct from extension, as has been fully explained in Part I of the *Principles*. And although philosophers have imagined a great many other motions, we however, who admit nothing that we do not conceive clearly and distinctly, must admit no motion except spatial motion, because we know clearly and distinctly that extension is capable of no other motion except spatial and that we can imagine no other motion.

But Zeno, it is said, denied spatial motion, and that for various reasons Diogenes the Cynic refuted in his own peculiar way, marching into the School where Zeno was expounding these principles and disturbing the audience by walking around. When he realized that he was being stopped by one of the listeners, to prevent him from walking about, he rebuked him thus: 'Why have you thus dared to refute your Master's reasoning?' However, to prevent anyone who is deceived by Zeno's

move after the lapse of half an hour, and if the speed is quadrupled, after the lapse of a quarter of an hour: and, if we conceive this speed increased to infinity, and the time reduced to instantaneity, then point A, at the greatest speed, will be at every instant, that is, constantly in the place from which it began to move, and so always remains in the same place; and what we know about point A must also be understood of all points of this wheel; and so all the points at this greatest speed constantly remain in the same place.

In reply, it must be observed that this argument is against the utmost speed of motion rather than against motion itself: however, we shall not examine here the correctness of Zeno's argument but we shall rather expose the misconceptions on which this entire argument is based, in so far as it proposes to refute motion. In the first place, then, he assumes that bodies can be conceived as moving with such speed that they cannot move faster. In the second place, that time is composed of instants, just as others have conceived that quantity is composed of indivisible points. Both assumptions are false. For we can never conceive a motion so swift that we cannot at the same time conceive a swifter one.

For it is contrary to our understanding to conceive a motion, describing a line however small, so swift that there cannot be a swifter one. And it is the same with slowness: for it implies the conception of a motion so slow that there cannot be a slower one.

We make the same assertion about time also, which is the measure of motion, that is, it is clearly contrary to our understanding to conceive such a time that there cannot be a shorter one. To prove all this, let us follow Zeno's procedure. Let us suppose then, as he did, a wheel ABC moving around its center with such speed that point A is at every moment at the place A from which it moves. I say that I clearly conceive a speed

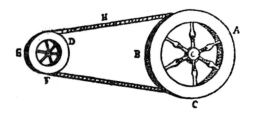

infinitely greater than this one and consequently smaller instants to infinity. For let it be assumed that, while the wheel ABC moves around its center, with the help of chord H, another wheel too, DEF (which I assume to be twice as small) moves around its own center. Now as wheel DEF is assumed to be twice as small as ABC, it is clear that wheel DEF moves twice as fast as wheel ABC; and consequently point D is, at instants twice as small, in the same place from which it began to move. Then, if we assign to wheel ABC the motion of wheel DEF, DEF will move four times faster than before (ABC); and if again we assign this speed of DEF to wheel ABC, then DEF will move eight times faster; and so on to infinity. But this seems quite clear from the mere conception of matter. For the essence of matter consists of extension or space always divisible, as we have proved; and there is no motion without space. We have also proved that one part of matter cannot at the same time occupy two spaces; for that would be tantamount to saying that one part of matter is equal to double the amount; as is evident from what has been proved above; therefore, if a part of matter moves, it moves through some space, and this space, however small it may be imagined to be, and consequently also the time through which that space is measured, will still be divisible, and consequently the duration or time of that motion will likewise be divisible, and that to infinity. Q.E.D.

Let us now proceed to another sophism, which is said to have been advanced by the same Zeno, as follows: If a body moves, it either moves in the place where it is, or where it is not. But not in the place where it is: for, if it is somewhere, it necessarily is at rest. Nor in the place where it is not. Therefore the body does not move. But this argument is just like the previous one; for it assumes that there is a time than which there is no shorter one; for if we answer Zeno that a body moves not in a place, but from the place where it is to the place where it is not; he will ask whether the body has not been in intermediate places. If we reply with this distinction: If by *has been* he means *has been at rest,* we deny that it was somewhere as long as it moved; but if by *has been* he means *has existed,* we say that as long as it moved, it necessarily existed; he will again ask: where did it exist, while it moved? If, finally, we answer: If by this *where it existed* he means *what place it occupied* while it moved, we say that it occupied no place; but if he asks *what place it left* we say that it left all the places that he wants to assign in the space through which it moved; he will continue to ask whether at the same instant it could occupy a place and change it. To which we finally reply with this distinction: If by an instant of time he means such a time that there cannot be a shorter one, he is asking an unintelligible question, as has been fully proved, and for that reason undeserving of a reply. But if he assumes time in the sense that I have explained above, that is, in its true sense, he can

75

never assign a time so small in which, however infinitely shorter it may be imagined, a body cannot occupy and change a place: a fact that is evident to one who is sufficiently observant. Hence it is quite clear, as we said above, that Zeno assumes a time so short that there cannot be a shorter one, and accordingly he proves nothing.

Apart from these two arguments, another argument still is attributed to Zeno, that may be read simultaneously along with the refutation in Descartes' *Letters,* the penultimate letter in volume I.

I should however like my readers to observe here that I have confronted Zeno's reasoning with my own reasoning; and so I have refuted him by Reason, not by the senses, as Diogenes did. For the senses cannot suggest to the searcher after truth anything but the Phenomena of Nature by which he is limited in the investigation of their causes; nor can they ever show the falsity of whatever the understanding comprehends clearly and distinctly as true. For that is how we judge and so this is our Method: to prove the things that we propose by reasons perceived clearly and distinctly by the understanding; considering as supererogatory whatever the senses tell us that seems contrary to them; as we have said, they can determine the understanding only in investigating one thing rather than another, but cannot convict it of falsity when it has perceived anything clearly and distinctly.

PROPOSITION VII

No body takes the place of another, unless at the same time this other body takes the place of some other body.

PROOF [1]

If it is denied, let it be assumed, if possible, that a body A takes the place of a body B, that I assume equal to A itself, and that does not leave its own place. Then the space that contained only B now contains (*by hypothesis*) A and B: and so double the corporeal substance that it previously contained, which (*by Proposition 4, Part II*) is absurd. Therefore no body takes the place of another body, and so on.

Q.E.D.

PROPOSITION VIII

When some body takes the place of another, at the same instant the place left by it is occupied by another body that touches it immediately.

PROOF

If the body B moves toward D the bodies A and C at the same instant will approach each other and touch each other, or not. If they approach and touch each other, the proposition is granted. But if they do not approach each other, and the entire space left by B

separates A and C, then a body equal to B (*by the Corollary to Proposition 2 and the Corollary to Proposition 4, Part II*) lies between them. But this body is not B (*by hypothesis*); therefore it is another body that at the same instant takes the place of B and, since it takes that place at the same instant, it cannot be anything else but a body that touches B immediately (*by the Scholium of Proposition* 6, *Part* II); for we have proved there that there is no motion from one place to another that does not require a time than which there can always be a shorter one. Hence it follows that the space of body B cannot be occupied at the same instant by another body which has to move through some space before occupying it. Therefore only the body that touches B immediately takes its place at the same instant.

Q.E.D.

SCHOLIUM

Since the parts of matter are really distant from each other (*by Article* 61, *Part* I *of the Principles*), one can be without the other (*by the Corollary to Proposition* 7, *Part* I) and they do not depend on each other. Therefore all these imaginative figments about Sympathy and Antipathy must be rejected as false. Furthermore, since the cause of any effect must always be positive (*by Axiom* 8, *Part* I), it must never be said that a body moves to prevent the existence of a void, but only from the impulsion of another body.

COROLLARY

In every motion there is a complete circle of bodies moving simultaneously.

PROOF

In the time that body 1 occupies the place of body 2, this body 2 must occupy the place of another, say 3, and so forth (*by Proposition 7, Part II*). Then at the same instant that body 1 occupied the place of body 2, the place left by body 1 must be occupied by another

body (*by Proposition 8, Part II*), say 8, or another that touches 1 itself immediately; since this occurs solely from the impulsion of another body (*by the Scholium of the preceding Proposition*), that is here assumed to be 1, all these bodies cannot move in the same straight line (*by Axiom 21*) but (*by Definition 9*) describe a complete circle.   Q.E.D.

PROPOSITION IX

If a circular pipe ABC is full of water, and if A is four times wider than B, in the time that the water (or any other fluid body) that is in A begins to move toward B, the water that is in B will move four times as fast.

PROOF

Since all the water that is in A moves toward B, as much water from C, which touches A immediately, must take its place (*by Proposition 8, Part II*); and from B an equal quantity of water must take the place of C (*by*

the same Proposition); therefore (*by Axiom* 14) it will move four times as fast.   **Q.E.D.**

What we say about a circular pipe must also be understood of all unequal spaces through which bodies that move simultaneously are forced to pass: the proof will be the same in the other cases.

LEMMA

If two semicircles are described from the same center, as A and B, the space between the perimeters will be everywhere equal. But if they are described from differ-

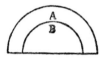 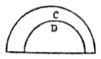

ent centers, as C and D, the space between the perimeters will be everywhere unequal. The proof is evident solely from the definition of a circle.

PROPOSITION X

A fluid body that moves through pipe ABC receives limitless degrees of speed.

PROOF

(*See the figure of the preceding Proposition*).

The space between A and B is everywhere unequal (*by the preceding Lemma*); therefore (*by Proposition* 9, *Part* II) the speed with which the fluid body moves through pipe ABC will be everywhere unequal. Further, since between A and B we conceive by thought infinite spaces always smaller and smaller (*by Proposition 5, Part II*), we also conceive, in infinite numbers, the inequalities that are everywhere, and hence (*by Proposition 9, Part II*), there will be infinite degrees of speed.

Q.E.D.

PROPOSITION XI

In a matter that flows through pipe ABC, there is a division into particles infinite in number.

PROOF

(*See figure in Proposition 9*).

The matter that flows through pipe ABC acquires at the same time infinite degrees of speed (*by Proposition 10, Part II*); therefore (*by Axiom 16*) it has infinite parts truly divided.

Read Articles 34 and 35, Part II of the *Principles.*

Q.E.D.

SCHOLIUM

Hitherto we have discussed the nature of motion; it is now necessary for us to investigate its cause, which is two-fold: namely, a first and general cause, that is the cause of all motions that there are in the universe, and a particular cause, by means of which it happens that the individual parts of matter acquire motions that they did not have previously. In regard to the general cause, since nothing must be admitted (*by Proposition 14, Part I and the Scholium of Proposition 17, Part I*) except what we perceive clearly and distinctly, and since we know clearly and distinctly no other cause except God (that is, the creator of matter), it is quite evident that no other general cause must be admitted except God. What we say here about motion, moreover, must also be understood of rest.

PROPOSITION XII

God is the principal cause of motion.

PROOF

See the Scholium immediately preceding.

PROPOSITION XIII

God still conserves by his co-operation the same quantity of motion and rest that he once implanted in matter.

PROOF

Since God is the cause of motion and rest (*by Proposition* 12, *Part* II); he conserves them still by the same power by which he created them (*by Axiom* 10, *Part* II); and in the same quantity as he first created them (*by Corollary to Proposition* 20, *Part* I).   Q.E.D.

SCHOLIUM

I. Although Theology declares that God accomplishes many acts through his good pleasure and in order to display his power to many, however, since those things that depend solely on his good pleasure are not known except by divine revelation, they must not be admitted in the Philosophy where only what Reason dictates is investigated, to avoid confusion between Philosophy and Theology.

II. Although motion is nothing else, in moving matter, but its mode, it still has a certain determined quantity: it will be clear from what follows how this quantity should be understood. Read Article 36, Part II of the *Principles*.

PROPOSITION XIV

Every thing, in as much as it is simple and undivided, and considered in itself alone, always persists in the same state, as much as it is in itself.

This Proposition is treated by many as an axiom: however, we shall prove it.

PROOF

Since nothing is in a particular state except through the co-operation of God alone (*by Proposition* 12, *Part* I); and since God is supremely consistent in his operations (*by Corollary to Proposition* 20, *Part* I); if we consider no external causes, that is, particular causes, but we view a thing only in itself, it will have to be asserted that, as far as it is in itself, it always persists in the state in which it is.   Q.E.D.

COROLLARY

A body that moves once always continues to move unless it is slowed down by external causes.

PROOF

This is evident from the preceding Proposition; however, to correct a misconception on motion, read Articles 37 and 38, Part II of the *Principles*.

PROPOSITION XV

Every moving body tends from itself to move continuously along a straight and not a curved line.

Although this Proposition might be classed among the Axioms, nevertheless I shall prove it from the preceding ones.

PROOF

Motion, having God only as cause (*by Proposition* 12, *Part* II), never has by itself any power to exist (*by Axiom* 10, *Part* I), but it is as it were procreated by God at every instant (*by what is proved of the Axiom just mentioned*). Therefore, as long as we consider solely the nature of motion, we shall never be able to assign to it duration, as belonging to its nature, one duration being able to be conceived greater than another. But if it is said that it is a property of the nature of a moving body to describe a curved line by its own motion, a greater duration would be assigned to the nature of motion than if it were assumed that it is in the nature of a moving body to tend to move continuously along a straight line (*by Axiom* 17). Now, since (as we have already proved) we cannot assign such duration to the nature of motion, we therefore cannot either postulate that it is in the nature of a moving body to move continuously along any curved line, but only along a straight line. Q.E.D.

SCHOLIUM

This proof will perhaps appear to many to show that it is no more in the nature of motion not to describe a curved line than a straight line; and that because no straight line can be assigned than which there cannot be a shorter one, either straight or curved, nor any curved line, than which too there cannot be another shorter curved line. However, although I take account of this, I consider that my proof is none the less correct: since it concludes from the universal essence alone, that is, from the essential difference of lines (not from the quantity of each one, that is, from an accidental difference) what was proposed for proof. But, not to make a point that is sufficiently clear by itself more obscure by demonstration, I refer Readers to the definition alone of motion, that affirms nothing more of motion than the transference of a part of matter from the vicinity, and so on, to the vicinity of other bodies, and so on. And so, unless we conceive this transference as the simplest possible, that it occurs along a straight line, we are assigning by a fiction something to motion that is not contained in its definition or essence and hence does not belong to its nature.

COROLLARY

From this Proposition it follows that every body, that moves along a curved line continuously, deflects from the line along which it would continue to move; and that by the force of some external cause (by Proposition 14, Part II).

PROPOSITION XVI

Every body that moves in a circular direction, as a stone, for example, in a sling, is continuously determined to move along the tangent.

PROOF

A body that moves in a circular direction is continuously prevented by an external force from moving in a straight line (*by the preceding Corollary*); if the force ceases, the body will of itself continue to move in a straight line (*by Proposition* 15). I say, in addition, that a body that moves in a circular direction is determined by an external cause to move along the tangent. For, if it is denied, let it be assumed, for example, that a stone in B, determined by a sling, moves not along tangent BD, but along another line from the same point and conceived outside or within the circle, as BF, when the sling is assumed to come from direction L toward B; or along BG (which I understand to make with line BH that is drawn from the center through the circumference and dissects it at point B, an angle equal to angle FBH), if on the contrary the sling is assumed to come from direction C toward B. But, if the stone at point B is assumed to be determined by the sling that moves in a circular direction from L toward B, proceeding to move toward F; necessarily (*by Axiom* 18) when the sling moves by a contrary determination from C toward K, the stone will be determined to move along the same line BF by a contrary determination and accordingly

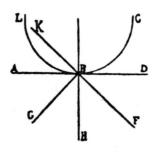

will tend toward K, not toward G: which is contrary to the hypothesis. And since[1] no line that can be drawn through point B, except the tangent, can be considered to make with line BH equal angles in the same direction, as DBH and ABH, there can be no line except the tangent that can validate the same hypothesis, whether the sling moves from L toward B or from C toward B; and consequently no line can be assumed except the tangent along which the stone tends to move.

Q.E.D.

ANOTHER PROOF

Instead of a circle, let a hexagon ABH be assumed, inscribed in a circle and a body C at rest on one side AB. Then suppose a ruler DBE (one end of which I assume fixed in center D and the other movable) moving around center D and continuously cutting line AB. It

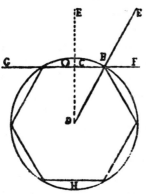

is clear that, if the ruler DBE, while it is conceived to be moving, meets body C at the moment when it cuts

[1] This is evident by Propositions 18 and 19 of Book 3 of the Elements.

line AB at right angles, the ruler itself will by its impulsion determine body C to continue to move along line FBAG toward G, that is, along the side AB extended to infinity. But since we have taken a hexagon arbitrarily, the same affirmation will have to be made of any other figure whatever that can, as we conceive, be inscribed in this circle; because, when C, at rest on one side of the figure, is impelled by the ruler DBE at the moment when it cuts that side at right angles, it will be determined by the ruler to move along that side extended to infinity. Let us therefore conceive, in place of the hexagon, a rectilinear figure with an infinite number of sides (that is, a circle, by Archimedes' definition); it is clear that the ruler DBE, when it meets body C, always meets it at the moment when it cuts at right angles some side of that figure; and so it will never meet body C without at the same time determining it to move along that side extended to infinity. And as any side extended in either direction must always fall outside the figure, this side extended to infinity will be tangent to the figure with an infinite number of sides, that is, a circle. And so if, in place of a ruler, we conceive a sling moving in a circular direction, it will continuously determine a stone to move steadily along a tangent.

Q.E.D.

It should here be noted that both proofs can apply to any curvilinear figure.

PROPOSITION XVII

Every body that moves in a circular direction tends to recede from the center of the circle that it describes.

PROOF

As long as any body moves in a circular direction, so long is it under compulsion of some external cause: at whose cessation it at once proceeds to move along a tangent (*by the preceding Proposition*), all whose points, except that which touches the circle, fall outside the circle (*by Proposition 16, Book 3 of the Elements*), and

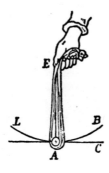

hence are further from the center. Therefore, when a stone, that moves in a circular direction in sling EA, is at point A, it tends to proceed along a line whose points are further from center E than all the points of the circumference LAB; which is nothing but a tendency to recede from the center of the circle that it describes.

Q.E.D.

PROPOSITION XVIII

If any body, say A, moves toward another body B at rest, and B does not lose any of its rest through the force of body A; then neither will A lose any of its motion, but will retain entirely the same amount of motion that it had previously.

PROOF

If it is denied, suppose body A loses its motion and yet does not transfer what it has lost into another body, say B; there will be in Nature, when that occurs, an amount of motion less than before, which is absurd

(*by Proposition* 13, *Part* II). The proof proceeds in like manner in respect of rest in body B; therefore, if one body does not transfer it to the other, B will retain all its rest and A all its motion.   Q.E.D.

PROPOSITION XIX

Motion, considered in itself, differs from its direction, impelling it toward one side or another; and it is not necessary for a moving body to be at rest for any length of time in order to be carried or repelled in an opposite direction.

PROOF

Suppose, as in the preceding Proposition, that a body A moves in a direct line toward B, and is prevented by body B from proceeding further; therefore (*by the preceding Proposition*) A will retain its motion intact, and will not be at rest for even the smallest space of time; however, when it proceeds to move, it will not move in the same direction toward which it moved previously, for it is assumed that it is prevented by B; therefore, its motion remaining intact, and its previous direction being lost, it will move in an opposite direction (*by*

90

what is said in Chapter 2 of the Dioptrics); and so (*by Axiom* 2) direction does not belong to the essence of motion, but differs from it, and the moving body, when repelled, is at no time at rest.   Q.E.D.

COROLLARY

Hence it follows that motion is not contrary to motion.

PROPOSITION XX

If body A meets body B, and carries it along with it, A loses from its motion as much motion as B acquires from A on account of its encounter with A.

PROOF

If it is denied, suppose that B acquires more or less motion from A than A loses; all that difference will have to be added or subtracted from the amount of motion of all Nature, which is absurd (*by Proposition* 13, *Part* II).

Therefore, since body B can acquire neither more nor less motion, it will acquire just as much as A loses.
          Q.E.D.

PROPOSITION XXI

If body A is twice as large as B, and moves with equal speed, A will have a motion twice as great as B, that is, a power to retain equal speed with B. (See the figure of the preceding Proposition.)

PROOF

Let us assume, for example, in place of A, twice B, that is (*by hypothesis*) A alone divided into two equal parts; each B has the power to remain in the position in which it is (*by Proposition 14 Part* II), and this power is equal in each one (*by hypothesis*). If now these two B's are joined, each retaining its own speed, there will be one A, whose power and amount will equal two B's, that is, double one B.   Q.E.D.

Note that this follows also from the definition of motion alone; for the greater a moving body is, the greater the matter that is separated from another matter; and therefore the separation is greater, that is (by Definition 8), the motion is greater. See our fourth Observation on the definition of motion.

PROPOSITION XXII

If body A equals body B, and A moves twice as fast as B, the power and motion in A will be double that of B. (See the figure in Proposition 20.)

PROOF

Suppose B, as soon as it has acquired a certain power of motion, has acquired four degrees of speed. If nothing approaches, it will proceed to move (*by Proposition 14, Part* II) and to persist in its position. Suppose now that it acquires from some new impulsion another new power equal to the first; it will therefore then acquire four new degrees of speed, in addition to the four previous ones, that it will also conserve (*by the same Propo-*

sition), that is, it will move twice as fast, that is, with a speed equal to A's and at the same time it will have double the power equal to A itself; therefore the motion in A is double that in B. Q.E.D.

Note that we here understand by power in moving bodies the amount of motion: an amount that in equal bodies must be greater in proportion to the speed of the motion, in so far as by that speed equal bodies are separated from bodies immediately tangential more than they would be at the same instant if they moved more slowly: and so (by Definition 8) they have also more motion. In bodies at rest by power of resistance is understood the amount of rest. Hence it follows:

COROLLARY I

The more slowly bodies move, the more they participate in rest; for they show more resistance to bodies moving more rapidly that meet them and have less power than they have, and they are also less separated from bodies that touch them immediately.

COROLLARY II

If body A moves twice as fast as body B, and body B is twice as big as A, there is as much motion in B, the greater, as in A, the smaller, and consequently also equal power.

PROOF

Let B be twice as big as A, and let A move twice as quickly as B, and further let C be twice as small as B and let it move twice as slowly as A; than B (*by Proposition 21, Part* II) will have a motion twice as great as C, and A (*by Proposition 22, Part* II) will have a motion twice as great as C; therefore (*by Axiom* 15) B and A have an equal motion: for the motion of each of them is twice the same third C.   Q.E.D.

COROLLARY III

From this it follows that *motion is distinct from velocity.* For we conceive that one of two bodies that have equal velocity can have more motion than the other (*by Proposition 21, Part* II); and inversely that bodies that have unequal speeds can have equal motion (*by the preceding Corollary*). This same corollary is also deduced from the definition of motion itself; for it is nothing but the transference of a body from the vicinity, and so on.

But it must here be noted that this third Corollary does not contradict the first. For velocity is conceived by us in two ways: either in so far as a body is separated more or less at the same time from bodies immediately touching it, and as such participates more or less in the motion or rest; or in so far as it describes a greater or smaller line at the same time and in this respect is distinct from motion.

I could have added here other Propositions in order to develop more fully Proposition 14, *Part* II *and to explain the powers of things in any state whatever, as we have here done in the case of motion; but it wll be sufficient to read Article* 43, *Part* II *of the Principles, and add only one Proposition that is necessary for the comprehension of what follows.*

PROPOSITION XXIII

When the modes of a body are forced to undergo a change, that change will always be the smallest possible.

PROOF

This Proposition follows clearly enough from Proposition 14, Part II.

PROPOSITION XXIV

Rule 1

If two bodies, say A and B (see the figure in Proposition 20), were quite equal and moved with the same speed in a straight line toward each other, when they meet, each will be deflected in the opposite direction without losing any part of its speed.

In this hypothesis it is quite clear that, to remove the opposition of these two bodies, either both must be deflected in opposite directions, or one must carry the other along with it; for they are opposed only in direction, but not in power of motion.

PROOF

When A and B meet, they must undergo some change (*by Axiom* 19) ; as moreover one motion is not opposed to the other motion (*by the Corollary to Proposition* 19, *Part* II) , they must lose none of their motion (*by Axiom* 19) . Therefore the change will occur in direction only; but we cannot conceive that the direction of one body only, say B, is changed, unless we assume (*by Axiom* 20) that A, by which it must be changed, is the stronger body. But this would be contrary to the hypothesis; therefore, since a change of direction cannot take place in one body only, it will take place in both, that is, A and B will be deflected in opposite directions *(by what is said in Chapter 2 of the Dioptrics)*, and will retain their motion intact. Q.E.D.

PROPOSITION XXV

Rule 2

If the bodies were unequal in volume, that is, B is greater than A, (see the figure in Proposition 20), other conditions being the same as before, then A only would be deflected, and both bodies would proceed to move with the same speed.

PROOF

Since A is assumed to be smaller than B, it will also have *(by Proposition 21, Part II)* less power than B; now, since in this hypothesis, as in the preceding one, there is opposition in the direction only, and so, as we have proved in the preceding Proposition, change must occur in direction only, it will occur only in A and not in B *(by Axiom 20)*; therefore only A will be deflected in an opposite direction by B, which is stronger, while retaining its own speed intact. Q.E.D.

PROPOSITION XXVI

If bodies are unequal in volume and speed, that is, B twice as large as A (see figure in Proposition 20), but the motion in A twice as fast as in B, other conditions being assumed as before, both bodies will be deflected in opposite directions, each one retaining the speed that it had.

PROOF

Since A and B move toward each other, according to the hypothesis, there is as much motion in one as in the other (*by Corollary to Proposition 22, Part* II); therefore the motion of one is not contrary to the motion of the other (*by Corollary to Proposition 19, Part* II), and the powers are equal in each (*by Corollary 2 to Proposition 22, Part* II). Therefore this hypothesis is altogether similar to the hypothesis of Proposition 24, Part II; and so by the same proof A and B will be deflected in opposite directions, while maintaining their own motion intact.

Q.E.D.

COROLLARY

From these three preceding Propositions it appears clear that the direction of a body requires, in order to change, the same power as the motion; hence it follows that a body that loses more than half of its direction and more than half of its motion undergoes more change than the body that loses all its direction.

PROPOSITION XXVII

Rule 3

If bodies are equal in volume, but B moves a little faster than A, not only will A be deflected in the opposite direction, but B also will transfer half of its speed, in

*which it exceeds **A**, to A and both will proceed to move
in the same direction with equal speed.*

PROOF

A *(by hypothesis)* is opposed to B not only by its direction, but also by its slowness, in so far as this slowness
participates in rest *(by the Corollary to Proposition 22,
Part II)*. Hence, although it is deflected in the opposite
direction and only its direction changes, all opposition
of those bodies is not on that account removed; therefore

(by Axiom 19) there must occur a change both in direction and in motion. But, since B by hypothesis moves
faster than A, B *(by Proposition 22, Part II)* will be
stronger than A; therefore *(by Axiom 20)*, a change will
arise in A from B, by which A is deflected in the opposite
direction. This was the first point.

Then, as long as A moves more slowly than B, it is
opposed to B *(by Corollary 1 to Proposition 22, Part II)*;
therefore the change must proceed *(by Axiom 19)* until
A does not move more slowly than B. But in this hypothesis no cause is so strong as to force A to move faster than
B; therefore since it can move neither more slowly than
B, since it is impelled by B, nor more quickly than B, it
will proceed to move with the same speed as B. Furthermore, if B transfers less than half of its excess speed to
A, then A will proceed to move more slowly than B; but
if B transfers more than half of its excess speed, then A
will proceed to move more quickly than B; both are
absurdities, as we have already proved. Therefore the
change will continue to the point where B transfers to

to A, still the force of direction A, is greater than the force of direction of C itself, moving from B toward A, and is as much greater as line BA is greater than line CA: for the greater line BA is than line CA, so much more time also (when B and A move with equal speed, as is here assumed) does B require to be able to move along line BD or CA, through which it is opposed to the direction of body A. And so, when C meets A obliquely from B, it will be directed, as though proceeding to move along line AB′ toward B′ (that I assume, when it is at the point where line AB′ cuts BC extended, is equidistant from C as C is from B). A, however, maintaining its motion and direction intact, will proceed to move toward C and will draw body B along with it, since B, as long as it is determined to move along diagonal AB′ and moves with the same speed as A, requires more time than A to describe a part of line AC by its motion, and to that extent is opposed to the direction of body A, that is stronger. But, in order that the force of direction of C itself moving from B toward A, in so far as it participates in line CA, may equal the force of direction of C itself moving directly toward A (by hypothesis, a power equal to A itself), necessarily B will have to have as many degrees of motion more than A as line BA is longer in extent than line CA and then, when it meets body A obliquely, A will be deflected in the opposite direction toward A′ and B toward B′, each of them maintaining its own motion intact. But if the excess of B over A is greater than the excess of line BA over line CA, then B will drive A toward A′ and will transmit to it so much of its own motion until the motion of B is in the same relation to the motion of A as line BA is to line CA while losing as much motion as it transferred to A, and it will proceed to move in the direction in which it previously moved. For example, if line AC is to line AB as 1 to 2, and the motion of body A to the motion of body B as 1 to 5, then B will transfer to A one degree of its motion, and will repel it in the opposite direction, and B with the remaining four degrees of motion will continue to move in the same direction in which it previously moved.

PROPOSITION XXVIII

Rule 4

If a body A (see figure in Proposition 27) is completely at rest and is a little larger than B, with whatever speed B moves toward A, B will never move A, but will be repelled by it in the opposite direction, while maintaining its own motion intact.

Observe that the opposition of these bodies is removed in three ways: either when one of them draws the other with it, and afterward they proceed to move in the same direction with the same speed; or when one is deflected in the opposite direction and the other retains its rest intact; or when one is deflected in the opposite direction and transfers some of its motion to the other body at rest; there is no fourth possibility (*by virtue of Proposition* 13, *Part* II). Therefore it will have to be proved now (*on account of Proposition* 23, *Part* II) that according to our hypothesis the change in these bodies is minimal.

PROOF

If B moved A until they both continued to move with the same speed, B (*by Proposition* 20, *Part* II) would

101

have to transfer as much of its power to A as A required, and (*by Proposition 21, Part* II) it would have to lose more than half of its motion, and consequently (*by the Corollary to Proposition 27, Part* II) more than half of its direction; and so (*by the Corollary to Proposition 26, Part* II) it would undergo more change than if it lost only its own direction. And if A loses some of its rest, but not so much as to continue finally to move with the same speed as B, then the opposition of these two bodies is not removed; for A will be opposed to the speed of B by its slowness, in so far as it participates in rest (*by the Corollary to Proposition 22, Part* II), and so B will have to be deflected in the opposite direction, and will lose all its direction and part of its motion, that it transferred to A; which is an even greater change than if it lost only its direction. The change therefore, following this hypothesis, will be, since it is in direction alone, the smallest that is possible in these bodies, and accordingly (*by Proposition 23, Part* II) no other will occur.

Q.E.D.

It must be observed in the proof of this Proposition that the same thing takes place in other cases: we have not in fact cited Proposition 19, Part II, in which it is proved that direction can be completely changed, while the motion itself remains nevertheless intact; care however must be taken that the power of direction is properly conceived. For in Proposition 23, Part II we did not say that the change will always be absolutely minimal, but the least possible. That a change, consisting solely in direction, can occur such as we have assumed in this proof, is clear from Propositions 18 and 19, Part II, with the Corollary.

PROPOSITION XXIX

Rule 5

If a body A at rest (see figure in Proposition 30) is smaller than B, however slowly B moves toward A, B will move it along with itself, transferring to it a part of its motion such that both then move with equal speed (Read Article 50, Part II of the Principles).

In this Rule also, as in the preceding one, only three cases can be conceived in which this opposition is removed; we shall prove by our hypothesis that the change in these bodies is minimal; and so (*by Proposition 23, Part* II) they must change in such a way.

PROOF

According to our hypothesis B transfers to A (*by Proposition* 21, *Part* II) less than half of its motion and (*by the Corollary to Proposition* 27, *Part* II) less than half of its direction. Now if B did not carry A along with it but was deflected in the opposite direction, it would lose its entire direction and a great change would occur (*by the Corollary to Proposition* 26, *Part* II) ; and much greater, if it loses all its direction, and at the same time a part of its motion, as is assumed in the third case; therefore according to our hypothesis the change is minimal.   Q.E.D.

PROPOSITION XXX

Rule 6

If a body A at rest were scrupulously equal to a body B moving toward it, it would partly be impelled by it, and partly repelled in the opposite direction.

Here too, as in the preceding Proposition, only three

cases can be conceived: and so it will have to be proved that we are here assuming the smallest possible change.

PROOF

If a body B carries a body A along with it, until both continue to move with the same speed, there will then be as much motion in the one as in the other (*by Proposition 22, Part* II), and (*by the Corollary to Proposition 27, Part* II) B will have to lose half of its direction and also (*by Proposition 20, Part* II) half of its motion. But if B is repelled by A in the opposite direction, then it will lose its entire direction, and will retain all its motion (*by Proposition 18, Part* II); a change that is equal to the previous one (*by the Corollary to Proposition 26, Part* II). But neither of these situations can occur; for, if A retained its state and could change B's direction, it would necessarily (*by Axiom* 20) be stronger than B, which would be contrary to the hypothesis. And if B carried A along with it until both moved with the same speed, B would be stronger than A, which is also contrary to the hypothesis. Since therefore neither of these two cases takes place, the third case therefore will occur, namely that B will impel A slightly and will be repelled by A.   Q.E.D.

Read Article 51, Part II of the *Principles.*

PROPOSITION XXXI

Rule 7

If B and A (see figure in the preceding Proposition) moved in the same direction, A more slowly than B, so that B finally reached A, and if A were greater than B, but the excess speed in B were greater than the excess size in A; then B would transfer to A so much of the motion that both would then advance with the same speed and in the same direction. But if on the other hand the excess size in A were greater than the excess speed in B, B would be deflected by it in the opposite direction, while maintaining all its motion intact.

Read Article 52, Part II of the *Principles*. Here again, as before, only three cases can be conceived.

PROOF

Part 1. B cannot be deflected in the opposite direction by A (*by Axiom* 20), for it is assumed (*by Propositions* 21 *and* 22, *Part* II) to be stronger than A; therefore, since B is stronger, it will move A along with it, and in such a way that both continue to move with the same speed. For a minimal change will occur, as is easily clear from what precedes.

Part 2. B cannot impel A (by Axiom 20) for it is assumed to be less strong than A (*by Propositions* 21 *and* 22, therefore (*by the Corollary to Proposition* 14, *Part* II) B will retain all its motion; not in the same direction, for it is assumed to be prevented by A; therefore (*by what has been said in Chapter 2 of the Dioptrics*) it will be deflected in the opposite direction, while maintaining its motion intact (*by Proposition* 18, *Part* II).

Q.E.D.

Observe that here and in the preceding Propositions we have assumed as proved that every body meeting another body directly is prevented absolutely by it from advancing further in the same direction and not in any other direction; to comprehend this, read Chapter 2 of the Dioptrics.

SCHOLIUM

So far, to explain the changes in bodies as a result of reciprocal impact, we have considered the two bodies as if separated from all bodies, without taking any account of those bodies that surround them on all sides. Now we shall consider the state and the changes in these bodies with respect to the bodies by which they are surrounded on all sides.

PROPOSITION XXXII

If a body B is surrounded on all sides by small moving bodies, impelling it at the same time with the same power in all directions, so long as no other cause intervenes, it will remain motionless in the same place.

PROOF

This Proposition is self-evident: for if it moved in any direction, by the impulsion of small bodies coming from one direction, these small bodies that move it would drive it with greater force than the other bodies that drive it at the same time in the opposite direction, and they cannot achieve their effect (*by Axiom* 20): which would be contrary to the hypothesis.

106

PROPOSITION XXXIII

A body B, under the same conditions as before, can, by the intervention of however small a force, move in any direction whatever.

PROOF

All bodies touching B immediately, because (*by hypothesis*) they are in motion and B (*by the preceding Proposition*) remains motionless, as soon as they touch B, will be deflected in the opposite direction, while maintaining their motion intact (*by Proposition* 28, *Part* II); and so body B is continuously and readily abandoned by the bodies touching it immediately; however great therefore B is conceived to be, no action is required to separate it from the bodies immediately touching it (*by our fourth Observation on Definition* 8). Therefore no external force, however small it may be, can impinge on B without being greater than the force that B has to remain in the same place (for we have already proved that it has no power itself to cling to bodies touching it immediately), and also, added to the impulsion of the small bodies driving B in the same direction as itself by an external force, without being greater than the force of the small bodies driving B in the opposite direction (for it was assumed equal to the contrary impulsion without external force); therefore (*by Axiom* 20) body B will move in any direction whatever by this external force, however small it may be.   Q.E.D.

PROPOSITION XXXIV

A body B, under the same conditions as before, cannot move faster than it is impelled by an external force, al-

though the particles by which it is surrounded are agitated far more quickly.

PROOF

The small bodies that at the same time as the external force drive B toward the same direction, although agitated much faster than the external force can move B, have not however *(by hypothesis)* a greater force than the bodies that drive B in the opposite direction, and will expend all their forces of direction only in resisting them, and will not transfer any speed to B *(by Proposition 32, Part* II) . Therefore, since no other circumstances or causes are assumed, B will not receive any speed from any other cause except external force, and accordingly *(by Axiom 8, Part* I) will not be able to move faster than the impulsion of an external force.   Q.E.D.

PROPOSITION XXXV

When a body B is so moved by an external impulsion, it receives most of its motion from the bodies by which it is continuously surrounded, not by an external force.

PROOF

B, however great it may be conceived to be, must move by an impulsion, however small *(by Proposition 33, Part* II). Let us conceive therefore that B is four times as great as the external body by whose force it is impelled; then, since *(by the preceding Proposition)* both must move with equal speed, there will be four times as much motion in B as in the external body by which it is impelled *(by Proposition 21, Part* II) ; therefore *(by Axiom 8,*

108

Part I) it does not have the principal part of its motion from the external force. And since no other causes are assumed except the bodies by which it is continuously surrounded (for B is assumed to be motionless by itself); *t* receives therefore (*by Axiom* 7, *Part* I) only from the bodies by which it is surrounded the principal part of its motion, not from an external force.   Q.E.D.

Observe that we cannot say here, as before, that the motion of the particles coming from one direction is required to resist the motion of particles coming from the opposite direction; for the bodies, moving with equal motion (as the assumption is) toward each other, are opposed by direction alone,[1] not by motion (by the Corollary to Proposition 19, Part II) and so give up only their direction, not their motion, in resisting each other; and for this reason B can receive no direction, and consequently (by the Corollary to Proposition 27, Part II) no speed, in so far as distinct from motion, from the bodies that surround it. But it receives motion; in fact, at the intervention of an external force it must necessarily be moved by them, as we have proved in this Proposition and as is clearly evident from the manner in which we have proved Proposition 33.

PROPOSITION XXXVI

If any body, for example our hand, can move in any direction whatever with equal motion so that it can in no way resist any bodies and no other bodies can resist it in any way, necessarily, in the space through which it

[1] See Proposition 24, Part II: for there it is proved that two bodies, by mutual resistance, give up their direction, not their motion.

thus moves, as many bodies will move in one direction as in any other direction whatever, with a force of speed equal to that of the hand.

PROOF

A body cannot move through any space that is not full of bodies (*by Proposition 3, Part* II). I say therefore that the space through which our hand can move thus is filled with bodies that will move under the same conditions that I have stated. For if that is denied, let it be assumed that they are at rest or that they move in some other way. If they are at rest, necessarily they will resist the motion of the hand (*by Proposition 14, Part* II) until its motion is communicated to them so that finally they move along with it in the same direction with equal speed (*by Proposition 20, Part* II). But in the hypothesis they are assumed not to resist; therefore these bodies move; *which is the first point.*

Furthermore, they must move in all directions. For if that is denied, let it be assumed that they do not move in some direction, say from A toward B. If therefore the hand moves from A toward B, necessarily it will encounter moving bodies (*by the first part of this proof*) and by our hypothesis with another direction different from that of the hand; therefore they will resist it (*by Proposition 14, Part* II) until they move along with the hand itself in the same direction (*by Proposition 24 and the Scholium of Proposition 27, Part* II). But they do not resist the hand (*by hypothesis*); therefore they will move in any direction whatever; *which was the second point.*

Again, these bodies will move in all directions with the same force of speed. For if it were assumed that they do not move with the same force of speed, and that the

odies moving from A toward B do not move with as
much force of speed as the bodies moving from A toward
C: then, if the hand moved from A toward B with the
same speed as the bodies move from A toward C (for it
is assumed to be able to move with equal motion in all

directions without resistance), the bodies moving from A
toward B will resist the hand (by *Proposition* 14, *Part* II)
until they move with the same force of speed as the hand
(by *Proposition* 31, *Part* II). But this is contrary to the
hypothesis; therefore the bodies will move with the same
force of speed in all directions; *which was the third point.*

Finally, if the bodies moved with a force of speed unequal to that of the hand, either the hand will move
more slowly or with less force of speed, or more quickly,
with a greater force of speed, than the bodies. In the
first case, the hand will resist the bodies following it in
the same direction (by *Proposition* 31, *Part* II). In the
latter case, the bodies that the hand follows and with
which it moves in the same direction will resist it (*by the
same Proposition*). Both alternatives are contrary to the
hypothesis. Therefore, since the hand can move neither
more quickly nor more slowly, it will move with the same
speed as the bodies.   Q.E.D.

*If it is asked, why I say with the same force of speed,
not absolutely with the same speed, read the Scholium of
the Corollary to Proposition 27, Part II. If it is then asked
whether, while moving for example from A toward B,
the hand does not resist the bodies moving at the same*

time from B toward A with the same speed, read Proposi-
tion 33, Part II, from which it will be understood that
their force is compensated by the force of the bodies (for
this force, by Part 3 of this Proof, is equal to the other)
that move at the same time with the hand from A toward
B.

PROPOSITION XXXVII

If any body, say A, can be moved by however small a
force in any direction whatever, it is necessarily sur-
rounded by bodies that move with the same speed for all
of them.

PROOF

The body A must be surrounded on all sides by bodies
(*by Proposition 6, Part II*), and those bodies move with
speed in any direction. For if they were at rest, A could
not be moved by however small a force in any direction
(as assumed) but only by such a force as could at least
move with it the bodies touching A immediately (*by
Axiom 20, Part II*). Then, if the bodies by which A is
surrounded were moved by a force greater in one direction than in another, say from B toward C rather than
from C toward B, as it is surrounded on all sides by moving bodies (*as we have already proved*); necessarily (*by
what we have proved in Proposition 33*) the bodies moving from B toward C would draw A along with them in
the same direction. And so no force, however small, will

be sufficient to move A toward B, but precisely a force
so great as to compensate the excess motion of the bodies

coming from B toward C (by *Axiom* 20) ; therefore they must move with the same force in all directions.

Q.E.D.

SCHOLIUM

Since these conditions occur in regard to bodies called Fluids, it follows that fluid bodies are those that are divided into many small particles moving with the same force in all directions. And, although those particles cannot be perceived even by the lynx-eyed, what we have just clearly proved cannot nevertheless be denied. For from what has been said in Propositions 10 and 11 such a subtle refinement of Nature is established as cannot be determined or reached by any thought (not to mention the senses). Furthermore, since it is also quite certain from what has been said that bodies resist other bodies solely by their being at rest and that in hardness, as the senses tell us, we perceive nothing else except that the parts of hard bodies resist the motion of our hands; we clearly deduce that those bodies, all whose particles are mutually at rest, are hard. Read Articles 54, 55, 56, Part II of the *Principles*.

PART III

Now that the most universal principles of the natural sciences have thus been expounded, we must now proceed to the exposition of the *Principles*. And from Article 20 to Article 43 the hypothesis is proposed that Descartes considers most suitable not only for the comprehension of the heavenly Phenomena, but also for the investigation of the natural causes.

Furthermore, since the best way to understand the nature of plants and man is to consider how they gradually arise and are generated from seeds, such principles will have to be thought out as are very simple and very easy to understand; and from which we may prove that the stars, the earth, and in short all that we find in this visible world could have arisen as though from certain seeds; although we know quite well that they never arose thus. For in this way we shall explain their nature far better than if we described them only as they are now.

I say that we are searching for simple principles, easy to understand; for unless they are such, we shall not require them; because we shall assume seeds in things for the sole reason that their nature may become known to us and in the manner of Mathematicians we may rise from the clearest things to more obscure one and from the most simple to the more complex.

Next we say that we are searching for such principles

from which to prove that the stars, the earth, and so on could have arisen. For we are not seeking such causes, as is generally the case with Astronomers, as are only sufficient to explain the Phenomena of the heavens; but such as lead us also to a knowledge of those things that are on the earth (because all things that we observe occurring on earth we judge should be included among the Phenomena of Nature). To find these principles, the following points must be observed in a good Hypothesis:

I. That it implies no contradiction (considered only in itself).

II. That it is as simple as possible.

III. That it is very easy to understand; which follows from the second condition.

IV. That everything that is observed in all Nature can be deduced from it.

We say finally that it is permissible for us to assume a Hypothesis from which as the cause we can deduce the Phenomena of Nature, although we know quite well that they did not arise thus. To make this clear, we shall use this example. If one finds traced on a paper the curved line called a Parabola, and one wants to investigate its nature, it is the same thing whether he assumes that the line was first a section of some Cone and then imprinted on the paper, or that it was traced by the movement of two straight lines, or produced in some other manner; provided that he deduces all the properties of the Parabola from what is assumed. Further, although he knows that the Parabola came from the impression of the section of the Cone on the paper, he will none the less be able to imagine at will another cause that seems most suitable to him to explain all the properties of the Parabola. So too, to explain the lines of Nature, it is permissible to assume a hypothesis at will, provided that we deduce therefrom by mathematical consequences all the Phenomena of Nature. And, what is more noteworthy, we shall scarcely be able to assume any hypothesis from which the same effects cannot be deduced, although more laboriously perhaps, by the Laws of Nature previously explained. For since by the aid of these Laws matter successively assumes all the forms of which it is capable; if we consider these forms in order, we shall finally be able to reach the form that is the form of this world; so that there is no error to be feared from a false hypothesis.

POSTULATE

It is asked that it be conceded that all this matter, of which this visible world is composed, was divided in the beginning by God into particles as equal as possible among themselves; not indeed into spherical particles, because many globules joined together do not fill a continuous space, but into parts shaped in another way, and of average size, that is, intermediary between all those of which heaven and the stars are composed; and that those particles had in themselves as much motion as is now found in the world, and that they moved equally: either individually around their own particular center, and mutually separated from each other, so as to constitute a fluid body, such as we conceive heaven to be: or several certain other points, equally distant from each other, and distributed in the same way as the centers of the fixed stars are now: and even around other somewhat greater centers that equal the number of the

Planets; and so they would compose as many different vortices as there are now stars in the world. See the figure in Article 47, Part 3 of the *Principles*.

This hypothesis considered in itself implies no contradiction: for it confers on matter nothing but divisibility and moton; and these modifications we have already previously proved exist really in matter; and, because we have shown that matter is infinite and that the matter of heaven and earth is one and the same, we can suppose without any risk of contradiction that the modifications have existed in all matter.

This hypothesis too is most simple, because it supposes no inequality or dissimilarity in the particles into which matter was divided in the beginning, nor even in their motion: whence it follows that this hypothesis is also very easy to understand. This is also clear from the fact that, by this hypothesis, nothing is assumed to have been in matter except of matter, namely divisibility and spatial motion.

That from this hypothesis itself all that is observed in Nature can be really deduced, we shall try to show, as far as possible, and that in the following order. First of all, we shall deduce the fluidity of the Heavens from this hypothesis, and we shall explain how it is the cause of light. Then we shall proceed to the nature of the Sun, and at the same time to what is observed in the fixed stars. After which we shall speak of the Comets, and lastly of the Planets and their Phenomena.

DEFINITIONS

I. By *Ecliptic* we understand that part of a vortex that, while revolving on its axis, describes the largest circle.

II. By *Poles* we understand the parts of a vortex that are most distant from the Ecliptic, that is, that describe the smallest circles.

III. By *Tendency to Motion* we understand not some thought but only that a part of matter is so situated and impelled to motion that it would really go in some direction if it were not prevented by any cause.

IV. By *Angle* we understand whatever in a body projects beyond the spherical shape.

AXIOMS

I. Many globules joined together cannot occupy a continuous space.

II. A portion of matter divided into angular parts, if its parts move round their own centers, requires a greater space than if all its parts were at rest and all their sides touched each other immediately.

III. The smaller a part of matter is, the more easily is it divided by the same force.

IV. Parts of matter that are in motion in the same direction, and in that motion do not recede from each other, are not actually divided.

PROPOSITION I

Parts of matter into which it was first divided were not round but angular.

PROOF

All matter was divided into equal and similar parts from the beginning (*by the Postulate*); therefore (*by*

Axiom 1 *and Proposition* 2, *Part* II) they were not round; and therefore they were angular (*by Definition* 4).

Q.E.D.

PROPOSITION II

A force that made the particles of matter move around their own centers, at the same time made the angles of the particles rub together on their meeting.

PROOF

All matter in the beginning was divided into equal (*by the Postulate*) and angular (*by Proposition* 1, *Part* III). If therefore, as soon as they began to move round their own centers, their angles had not been rubbed away, necessarily (*by Axiom* 2) all matter would have had to occupy a greater space than when it was at rest; but this is absurd (*by Proposition* 4, *Part* II); therefore their angles were rubbed away as soon as they began to move.

Q.E.D.

Thoughts on Metaphysics

Appendix: Part I

containing

Metaphysical Speculations

Wherein are briefly explained the principal questions that commonly arise in the general field of Metaphysics concerning Being and its affections.

CHAPTER 1

True Being, False Being, and Being deduced by Reason

I say nothing about the definitions of this science nor even about the matter of which it treats. My intention is solely to explain here the points that are rather obscure and are discussed by authors in their metaphysical writings.

Definition of Being

Let us begin therefore with Being, by which I understand: All that, when perceived clearly and distinctly, we find necessarily existing or at least potentially existing.

A Chimera, an Imaginary Being, and a Being deduced by Reason are not Beings

From this definition, or if it is preferred, from this description, it follows that a *Chimera, an Imaginary Being,* and a *Being deduced by Reason* can in no sense be accepted among beings. For a Chimera[1] by its very nature cannot exist. As for an *Imaginary Being,* it excludes clear and distinct perception; because man, from the mere use of freedom alone, and not unwittingly, as in the case of error, but purposely and knowingly, joins together what he wishes to join and disunites what it pleases him to disunite. Finally, a *Being deduced by Reason* is nothing but a way of thinking, that serves *to retain, explain,* and *imagine* more easily things that are known. It should be observed now that by a way of thinking we understand what we have already explained in the Scholium to proposition 4, Part I; namely, all the affections of thought, such as understanding, joy, imagination, and so on.

In What Ways of Thinking We Retain Things

That there are certain ways of thinking that serve *to retain* things more firmly and more easily, and to recall them to mind whenever we so desire, or to retain them in our mind, is sufficiently well established for those who use that well known rule of memory; to remember a totally new item and to imprint it on the memory, we resort to another item that is familiar to us, and that has identity with this one either in name only or in reality. In a similar manner the Philosophers have arranged all

[1] Observe that by the expression Chimera here and in what follows is understood that of which the nature involves an apparent contradiction, as is fully explained in Chapter 3.

natural things in certain categories to which they have recourse to them, that they call genus, species, and so on.

In What Ways of Thinking We Explain Things

To explain a thing, we have also ways of thinking; we determine it by comparison with something else. The ways of thinking that we use for this purpose are called *time, number, measurement,* and whatever others there may be. Of those mentioned, time serves to explain duration; number, the separation of quantity; measurement, the continuity of quantity.

In What Ways of Thinking We Imagine Things

Lastly, as we are accustomed, every time we know things, to represent them also by some image in our imagination, it happens that we *imagine* positively non-beings as beings. For the mind, considered solely in itself, in so far as a thinking thing, does not have a greater power to affirm than to deny; but since imagination is nothing but sensation of those traces found in the brain as a result of the movement of spirits, a movement that is aroused in the senses by objects, such sensation cannot be other than a confused affirmation. Hence it happens that we imagine as beings all the modes that the mind uses for denial; such as *blindness, extremity* or *finality, terminus, darkness,* etc.

Why The Beings Deduced by Reason Are Not Ideas of Things and Yet Are so Considered

Hence it is clearly evident that these ways of thinking are not ideas of things and cannot in any sense be classed as ideas; and so too they have no idea that necessarily exists or can exist. But the reason why these ways of thinking are considered as ideas of things is that they spring and arise from ideas of things so immediately as to be confused very readily with them by those who are not scrupulously alert. That is why also names have been assigned to them as if to signify beings that exist outside our own mind and why these beings, or rather these non-beings, have been called Beings deduced by Reason.

False Distinction Between Real Being And Being Deduced by Reason

From what precedes it is easy to see how inept is the division that separates Being into Real Being and Being deduced by Reason. For Being is thus divided into Being and Non-Being, or into Being and Mode of Thinking. However I am not surprised that Philosophers who are concerned with words or grammar fall into such errors: for they judge things by names, not names by things.

How Being Deduced by Reason can be Termed Mere Nothingness and How it can be Termed Real Being

No less unreasonable is the man who asserts that Being deduced by Reason is not mere Nothingness. For if he seeks for the significance of these terms beyond his understanding, he will find that it is mere Nothingness. If on the contrary he understands the ways of thinking themselves, they are Real Beings. For when I ask what a *species* is, I am merely asking the nature of this way of thinking that is really a Being and is distinct from any other way of thinking. But these ways of thinking cannot be called ideas and cannot be called either true or false, just as love cannot be called true or false, but good or

ad. So when Plato said that man is a biped animal
without feathers he did not commit a greater error than
those who said that man is a rational animal. For Plato
knew, as well as others know, that man is a rational
animal. But he classified man in a particular category
so that, whenever he wanted to think of man, he would
instantly encounter the thought of man by referring to
the category that he could remember easily. Moreover
Aristotle was very gravely mistaken if he thought that he
had adequately explained the essence of man by his own
definition. Whether Plato acted properly might be questioned. But this is not the place for such a discussion.

In an Investigation of Things, Real Beings are not to be Confused with Beings Deduced by Reason

From all that has been said before, it is evident that
there is no agreement between a Real Being and the objects represented by the Beings deduced by Reason.
Hence it is easy to see how carefully we must guard, in
the investigation of things, against confusing Real Beings
with Beings deduced by Reason. For there is a difference
between inquiring into the nature of things and inquiring into the ways in which we perceive them. If these
two processes are confused, we shall be able to understand neither the ways of perception nor the nature itself; besides, and this is a very serious matter, we shall
fall into grave errors, as has hitherto been the case with
many.

How to Distinguish Between the Being Deduced by Reason and the Imaginary Being

It should also be observed that many have confused
Being deduced by Reason with Imaginary Being. They

believe that Imaginary Being is also Being deduced [
Reason, because it has no existence outside the min
But if one carefully considers the definitions just pr
posed of Being deduced by Reason and Imaginary Bein
a great difference between them will be discovered, n
only in respect of their cause, but also as a result of the
nature, without respect to their cause. For we saw th
Imaginary Being is nothing but two *termini* conjoin
solely by the will without any guidance by Reaso
Hence Imaginary Being may by accident be true. B
Being deduced by Reason neither depends on the w
alone, nor is it composed of any *termini* mutually co
joined, as is sufficiently evident from the definition.
anyone then asks whether Imaginary Being is Re
Being, or Being deduced by Reason, we must repeat a
assert only that we have already said, that the divisi
of Being into Real Being and Being deduced by Reas
is bad. For that reason the question whether Imagina
Being is Real Being or Being deduced by Reason
founded on no valid basis; for it is assumed that a
Beings are divided into Real Beings and Beings deduc
by Reason.

Division of Being

But let us return to our proposed topic, from whic
we seem to have digressed to some extent. From th
definition of Being, or, if one prefers, from the defin
tion already given, it is easy to see that a Being must I
divided into a being that exists necessarily by its ow
nature, that is, whose essence involves existence, an
into a being whose essence involves only a *possible* e
istence. This latter being is divided into Substance an
Mode, whose definitions are given in Part I of the *Pri*

les of Philosophy, articles 51, 52 and 56; it is therefore
t necessary to repeat them here. I only want this to be
served in regard to this division, that we expressly
te: A Being is divided into Substance and Mode, but
t into Substance and Accident; for the Accident is
thing more than a way of thinking, since it denotes
ly a respect. For example, when I say that a triangle
oves, the motion is not a mode of the triangle but of
e body that moves. Hence in respect of the triangle
e motion is called an Accident, but in respect of the
dy the motion is a real being, or a mode. For the
otion cannot be conceived without the body but it
n be so conceived without the triangle.

Moreover, to clarify the comprehension of what has
ready been said and also of what follows, we shall at-
mpt to explain what must be understood by *the being*
essence, the being of existence, and lastly *the being*
power. Our motive is the ignorance of certain persons,
ho recognize no distinction between essence and exist-
ce or, if they do so, confuse *the being of essence* with
e *being of the idea* or *the being of power.* To satisfy
em and to elucidate the question itself we shall ex-
ain the problem as distinctly as we can in the follow-
g chapter.

CHAPTER 2

he Nature of the Being of Essence, of the Being of Ex-
istence, of the Being of Idea, of the Being of Power

To obtain a clear perception of the meaning of these
ur *beings,* it is only necessary to set before us what we

have said about the uncreated substance, that is Go namely:

Creatures are Eminently in God

1. God contains eminently what is found formally i created things, that is, God has such attributes that a created things are contained therein in a more emine way; *see Part I, Axiom 8 and Corollary I to Propositic* 12. For example, we clearly conceive extension withou any existence and so, since it has by itself no power exist, we proved that it was created by God (*Last Pr position, Part I*). And, because there must be in the cau as much perfection at least as in the effect, it follows tha all the perfections of extension are in God, since v afterward saw that the extended thing was by its natu divisible, that is, contains an imperfection, we could n consequently attribute extension to God (*Part I, Pr position* 16), and so we were compelled to admit tha there is in God some attibute that contains all the im perfections of matter in a more excellent form (*Scholiu to Proposition 9, Part I*), and that can take the place o matter.

2. God knows Himself and all other things; that i He has also in Himself all things objectively (*Part Proposition 9*).

3. God is the cause of all things, and He operate through the absolute fredom of His will.

The Nature of the Being of Essence, of Existence, o Idea, and of Power

So it is clearly to be seen from this what we mean b these four *beings*.

First of all, *the being of essence* is nothing more tha

the manner in which created things are comprehended in the attributes of God. Secondly, *the being of idea* is so called in so far as all things are contained in the idea of God. Then *the being of power* is so called with regard to the power of God, by which He had been able to create by the absolute freedom of His will all that did not exist until then. Lastly, *the being of existence* is the essence itself of things outside God and considered in itself, and it is attributed to things after their creation by God.

These Four Beings are not Distinguished from each other except in Created Things

From this it is quite clear that these four beings are distinguished from each other only in created things, but in no respect in God. For we do not conceive that God was in power in another being and His existence and His understanding are not distinguished from His essence.

Reply to Certain Questions on Essence

From these conclusions we can easily reply to the questions that are frequently raised on the subject of essence. These questions are as follows: *Is essence distinct from existence? If it is distinct, is it something different from idea? If it is something different from idea, does it have some existence beyond the understanding?*

This last point must necessarily be admitted. Now to the first question on the distinction we reply that in God the essence is not distinct from the existence, since without existence essence cannot be conceived; in the other beings the essence differs from existence, for the former can be conceived without the latter. To the second question we reply that a thing that is perceived beyond the understanding clearly and distinctly, that is, truly, is something different from an idea. But a final question is posed: *Is the being beyond the understanding something by itself or is it created by God?*

Our answer is that formal essence is not by itself, nor is it created; for these two assertions would imply that a thing exists in action, but that it depends solely on the divine essence, in which all things are contained. And so in this sense we concur with those who say that the essences of things are eternal. It might still be asked: *How do we know the essence of things before knowing the nature of God?;* since those essences, as we have just said, depend solely on the nature of God. To this I reply that this arises from the fact that things are already created; for if they were not created, I would wholeheartedly agree that this knowledge would be impossible without a previous adequate knowledge of the nature of God. Likewise it would be impossible, even more impossible, to know the nature of the ordinates without knowing the nature of the Parabola.

Why the Author in his Definition of Essence Resorts to the Attributes of God

It must further be observed that, although the essences of the non-existing modes are comprehended in their substances, and their *being of essence* is in their substances, we have nevertheless wished to resort to God in order to explain in a general sense the essence of the modes and substance, and also because the essence of the modes was not in their substance until these substances were created and until we sought the eternal *being of the essences.*

Why the Author has not Examined the Definitions Proposed by Others

I do not think it worthwhile to refute here the authors whose opinions differ from ours, or to examine their definitions or descriptions of essence and existence; for in this way we should be making more obscure what is now clear. For what is clearer than understanding what essence and existence are? Since we cannot attach any definition to a thing without at the same time explaining its essence.

How to Learn Easily the Distinction between Essence and Existence

Finally, if any Philosopher still doubts whether essence is distinct from existence in created things, he has no reason to exert himself much to banish this doubt about the definitions of essence and existence. For if he merely approaches any sculptor or wood carver, they will show him how they conceive in a certain orderliness a statue that does not yet exist and afterward they will present it to him as existing.

CHAPTER 3

The Meaning of Necessary, Impossible, Possible, and Contingent

What we must here Understand by Affections

Having thus explained the nature of being in so far as it is being, we pass on to the explanation of some affections of being; where it is to be observed that by *affections* we understand here what Descartes has elsewhere designated as *attributes* in Part I, *Philosophical Principles,* article 52. For Being, in so far as it is a being, does not affect us by itself, as a substance. It must therefore be explained by some attribute, from which however it differs only by the distinction of Reason.

I cannot therefore be sufficiently surprised at the excessively subtle ingenuities of those who have sought, not without great detriment to the truth, an intermediary between Being and Nothingness. But I shall not stop to refute their error, since they themselves, when they try to give definitions of such affections, dissipate themselves completely in their own vain subtleties.

Definitions of Affections

We shall therefore pursue our subject and state that the *affections* of Being are *certain attributes,* under which we know *the essence or the existence of every being,* from which however they are not distinct except by a distinction of Reason. Certain of these affections I shall try to explain here (for I am not understanding to treat all of them) and to distinguish them from the denominations that are not the affections of any being. And first of all I shall discuss the meaning of *necessary* and impossible.

In How Many Ways a Thing is Said to be Necessary and Impossible

A thing is said to be necessary and impossible in two ways; either in respect of its essence, or in respect of its cause. In respect of the essence, we know that God exists necessarily; for His essence cannot be conceived without existence. But a Chimera in respect of the contradiction contained in its essence exists. In respect of the cause, things, for example material things, are said to be impossible or necessary; for if we consider only their essence, we can conceive it clearly and distinctly without existence. For this reason they can never exist by the force and necessity of their essence, but only by the force of their cause, that is, God, the creator of all things. Therefore, if it is the divine decree that a thing exist, it will exist necessarily; if not, it will be impossible for it to exist. For it is self-evident that a thing that has no cause, either internal or external, for existence, cannot possibly exist. But in this second hypothesis a thing is considered of such a nature that neither by the force of its essence, which is what I understand by internal cause, nor by the force of the divine decree, the eternal and sole cause of all things, can it exist. Hence it follows that it is impossible for things such as we have assumed in the second hypothesis to exist.

How the Chimera can be Called a verbal Being

It must here be observed:

1. That a Chimera, being neither in the understanding nor in the imagination, can properly be called a Verbal Being; for it cannot be expressed except by words. For example, we express in words a squared circle, but we cannot in any way imagine it and still less can we understand it. Therefore a Chimera is nothing but a word, and so Impossibility cannot be numbered among its affections of being, for it is a simple negation.

Created Things, in as much as Essence and Existence, Depend on God

2. It must be observed that not only the existence of created beings, but also, as we shall prove later in the second part with the most convincing evidence, their essence and nature depend solely on the decree of God. Hence it clearly follows that created things have not of themselves any necessity, since they have no essence by themselves and do not exist by themselves.

The Necessity that is in Created Things by a Cause is Related to their Essence or their Existence, but in God these two Things are not Distinct

3. It must be observed that the necessity such as is in created things by the power of the cause is said to be so in respect of their essence or in respect of their existence: for these two are distinct from each other in created things. For essence depends on the eternal laws of nature, while existence depends on the succession and order of causes. But in God, whose essence is not distinct from His existence, the necessity of the essence also is not distinct from the necessity of existence. Hence it follows that, if we conceived the entire order of Nature, we should find that many things, whose nature we perceive clearly and distinctly, that is, whose essence is necessarily such and such, could in no manner exist; for we should find that it is as impossible for such things to exist in Nature as we know it at present as it is impossible for a huge elephant to be able to pass through the eye of a needle; although we clearly perceive the nature of both. Hence the existence of those things would be merely a Chimera, that we could neither imagine nor understand.

Possibility and Contingency are not Affections of Things

4. To these observations on necessity and impossibility it has seemed fitting to add a few words on *possibility* and *contingency*; for these two concepts are considered by some as affections of things, although they are really nothing but defects in our understanding. This I shall show clearly after explaining the meaning of these two terms.

The Meaning of Possible and of Contingent

A thing is said to be *possible when we know its efficient cause and yet are unaware whether it is a determined cause.* Hence we can consider it as possible, but not as necessary or impossible. If however we consider the *essence of a thing simply, but not its cause,* we shall call it *contingent;* that is, we shall consider it, so to speak, as intermediary between God and a Chimera; because we do not find in it, considered from the viewpoint of essence, any necessity for existence, as in the divine essence, or any contradiction or impossibility, as in a Chimera. But if anyone wants to call *contingent* what I term *possible* and on the other hand *possible* what I call *contingent,* I shall not contradict him; for I am not accustomed to dispute about names. It will be sufficient to grant that these two terms are nothing but defects in our perception and not something real.

Possibility and Contingency are only Defects of our Understanding

If anyone should want to deny this, his error can be proved without any difficulty. For if he considers Nature, and how it depends on God, he will find nothing *con-*

tingent in things, that is, nothing that, considered as a thing, can exist or not exist, or, to use the popular idiom, that is *really* contingent. This is readily evident from what we have explained in Axiom 10, Part I: As much force is required to create a thing as to conserve it. Therefore no created thing does anything by its own power, just as no created thing begins to exist by its own power. From which it follows that nothing happens except by the power of the all-creating cause, that is, God, who by his intervention procreates all things every moment. Since nothing happens except by the divine power alone, it is easy to see that those things that happen occur by the power of God's decree and by His will.

But, since there is no inconsistency or change in God (*by Proposition 18 and Corollary to Proposition 20, Part I*), He must have decreed from all eternity that He would produce those things that He now produces; and, since nothing is more necessary than the existence of what God has decreed should exist, it follows that the necessity of existence has been since all eternity in all created things. Nor can we say that those things are contingent, because God could have decreed otherwise. For since in eternity *when* does not exist, nor *before,* nor *after,* or any temporal affection, it follows that God did not exist before those decrees so as to be able to decree otherwise.

Reconciliation of Freedom of our Will with the Predestination of God Transcends Human Comprehension

In regard to the freedom of the human will, that we have asserted is free (*Scholium to Proposition 15, Part I*), it too is conserved by God's intervention, and no man wishes anything or does anything except what God has since eternity decreed that he should wish or do. How that is possible, with the maintenance of human freedom, transcends our comprehension. Nor should we for that reason reject on account of our ignorance what we clearly perceive. For we know clearly and distinctly, if we consider our own nature, that we are free in our actions and that we deliberate on many of them for the sole reason that we want these actions. If we also consider the nature of God, as we have just shown, we clearly and distinctly perceive that everything depends on Him and that nothing exists except that of which the existence has been decreed by God since eternity. How the human will is procreated by God every single moment in such a fashion as to remain free, that we know not. For there are many things that transcend our understanding and yet we know that they were performed by God; for example, that real division of matter into infinite particles was proved by us with sufficient evidence (*in Part* 2, *Proposition* II), although we do not know how that division arose. Observe that we assume here as a known fact that these two notions, *possibility* and *contingency,* signify only a defect in our knowledge of the existence of a thing.

CHAPTER 4

Duration of Time

From the division of Being that we made above into being whose essence involves existence and into being whose essence involves only possible existence, arises the distinction between eternity and duration.

What Eternity is

Of *eternity* we shall speak at greater length later on. At this point we shall say only that it is the *attribute under which* we conceive the infinite existence of God.

What Duration is

Duration is the *attribute under which we conceive the existence of created things,* in so far as they persist *in their actuality.* From this it clearly follows that between duration and the entire existence of anything there is no distinction except that of Reason.

For whatever you withdraw from the duration of a thing must necessarily be withdrawn from its existence. To determine duration, we compare it with the duration of those things that have an unvarying and determined motion and *this comparison* is called *time.*

What Time is

Time therefore is not an affection of things, but only a simple way of thinking, or, as we have already stated, a being deduced by Reason: it is a way of thinking that serves to explain duration. Here it must be observed, in regard to duration,—and this will later on be serviceable when we discuss eternity—that duration is conceived as greater and smaller, as though composed of parts, and finally that it is an attribute of existence only, not of essence.

CHAPTER 5

Opposition, Order, etc.

From the fact that we compare things with each other, certain notions arise that, however, are nothing, outside the things themselves, but ways of thinking. This is evident because, if we wish to consider them as things placed outside thought, we instantly confuse a clear concept that we have of them elsewhere. Such are the notions of *Opposition, Order, Agreement, Diversity, Subject, Complement* and whatever other notions similar to these there may be.

What are Opposition, Order, Agreement, Diversity, Subject, Complement, etc.

These things, I assert, are perceived clearly enough by us, as long as we conceive them, not as something distinct from the essences of things opposed, classified, etc., but only as modes of thinking by which we retain or imagine more easily the things themselves. Therefore I do not consider it necessary to discuss them at greater length at this point, but I proceed to the terms commonly called transcendental.

CHAPTER 6

One, the True, the Good

These terms are considered by almost all Metaphysicians as the most general Affections of Being. For they say that all Being is One, True, and Good, although nobody thinks it. But we shall see what they mean by these terms when we have examined each of them separately.

What Oneness is

Let us begin therefore with the first, namely, One. They say that this term signifies something real beyond the understanding; but they cannot explain what this adds to being. This clearly shows that they confuse beings deduced by Reason with Real Being; hence they create confusion out of what they understand clearly. Now we assert that *Oneness* is in no sense distinct from the thing, or adds nothing to being, but is only a mode of thinking, by means of which we separate one thing from other things that are similar to it or agree with it in some manner.

What Plurality is and in what Respect God can be Said to be One and in what Respect Unique

To Oneness is opposed Plurality, which certainly adds nothing to things, and is nothing but another mode of thinking, as we know clearly and distinctly. Nor do I see what remains to be said further about a subject that is clear. Only this should be observed here, that God, in so far as we distinguish Him from other beings, can be said to be *One*; but, in so far as we conceive that there cannot be several with the same nature, He is called *unique*. But, if we wanted to examine the question more carefully, we could perhaps show that God is not called one and unique except incorrectly. But it is not such an important matter; in fact, it is actually of no importance, to those who are concerned with them, not with names. Therefore, leaving this question, we pass on to the next one and we shall explain in the same way what false is.

What False is, What True is, both to the People and to the Philosopher

To acquire a proper conception of these two notions, *true* and *false,* we shall begin with the significance of the words; from which it will be apparent that they are nothing but the external denominations of things, and cannot be assigned to them except in a rhetorical sense. But since the people first discovered words, that are afterward used by Philosophers, it seems to be the province of the person who searches for the first significance of a word to ask what it first meant to the people; especially in the absence of other causes that could be drawn from the nature of language for such an investigation. The first meaning therefore of *true* and *false* seems to have originated from stories; and a story was said to be true that described an incident that had actually occurred; false, that described an incident that had not occurred anywhere at all. Afterward Philosophers used this term to denote agreement or non-agreement of an idea with its object. Therefore an idea is called True when it shows us a thing as it is in itself. False when it shows us a thing otherwise than it is in reality. Ideas are, in fact, nothing but stories or mental histories of nature. And hence there was later on a metaphorical transference to inert things; as when we say that gold is true or false, as if the gold presented to us told us something about itself that is in it, or not.

True is not a Transcendental Term

Those persons therefore are quite deceived who have considered *true* a transcendental term or an affection of Being. For it cannot be applied to things themselves except incorrectly, or, if you prefer, rhetorically.

The Difference Between Truth and a True Idea

If one asks further what truth is apart from a true idea, one may also ask what whiteness is apart from a white body: for these things are related to each other in the same way.

The cause of True and the cause of False we have already discussed previously: therefore nothing remains to be observed here nor would it have been worth while to observe what we have said, if writers had not been so involved in similar fatuities as not to be able to extricate themselves afterward in their search everywhere for trouble where there is none.

What are the Properties of Truth? Certainty is not in Things

The properties of truth or of an idea are true.

1. Because it is clear and distinct.

2. Because it banishes all doubt, by a single word, as to its certainty. Those who seek certainty in things themselves are deceived in the same way as when they seek Truth in them. And although we say *A thing is uncertain,* we take the object for the idea, as orators do, just as when we say that *A thing is doubtful:* unless perhaps we understand by uncertainty either the thing that induces uncertainty or the doubt in us. Nor is

there any need to dwell any longer on these questions. Therefore we shall proceed to the third term, and at the same time we shall explain what its contrary means.

Good and Bad are so Called Only Relatively

A thing considered by itself is said to be neither *good* nor *bad,* but only in relation to another thing, to which it is useful or harmful in securing what it likes. And so every single thing may be said to be good and bad in different respects and at the same time. Thus, for example, Ahitophel's advice to Absalom is called good in the Holy Scriptures: yet it was bad for David, whose death it presaged. But many other things are good that are not good for all: thus, salvation is good for men, but it is neither good nor bad for animals or plants with which it has no relation. God is called supremely good, because He is beneficial to all: by His intervention He conserves the being of everyone, than which nothing is more beloved. Nothing can be absolutely bad, as is self-evident.

Why Some Have Granted a Metaphysical Good

Those who are in quest of a metaphysical good that lacks every relation labor under a false preconception: because they confuse a distinction of Reason with a Real or Modal distinction. For they distinguish between a thing itself and the tendency that is in everything to conserve its being, although they do not know what they mean by tendency. For between these two concepts, although they are distinguished by Reason or rather by words,—a fact that has especially led to error—there is really no distinction whatever.

143

How to Distinguish Things and the Tendency by Virtue of which they tend to Persist in their own State

To make it clearly understood, we shall present an example of something very simple. Motion has the power of persisting in its state. This power is certainly nothing but the motion itself, that is, the nature of motion is such.

For if I say that in this body A there is nothing else but a certain amount of motion, it clearly follows from this, so long as I consider this body A, that I must always say that this body moves. For if I said that this body has lost by itself its power of motion, I should necessarily atttribute to it something more than what we assumed in the hypothesis, and thus it would lose its nature.

But if this reasoning seems rather obscure, let us agree then that this tendency to move is something beyond the laws themselves and the nature of motion: since therefore it is assumed that this tendency is a metaphysical good, this tendency will also necessarily have in itself a tendency to persist in itself and this tendency in turn will have another and so on to infinity. Which is the greatest absurdity imaginable.

Now the Reason why some distinguish the tendency from the thing itself is that they find in themselves a desire to conserve themselves and imagine such a desire in everything.

Whether God may be Called Good before the Creation of Things

The question however is asked whether God can be called good before He created things. From our definition it seems to follow that God did not have such an attribute, because we say that a thing, considered in itself, can be called neither good nor bad. Now this will appear absurd to many: but on what grounds, I do not know. For we affirm of God many attributes of this kind that, before the creation of things, did not apply to Him, except in regard to power: as when He is called creator, judge, all-merciful, etc. Therefore such arguments ought not to delay us.

How Perfect Can be so Called Relatively and how it can be Called Absolutely

Furthermore, just as good and bad can be predicated only relatively, so too with perfection, except when we take perfection for the essence itself of a thing, in which sense, as we said previously, God has infinite perfection, that is, infinite essence, or infinite being.

It is not my intention to add anything more to this: for I think that the rest of what relates to the general field of Metaphysics is well enough known: and hence it is not worthwhile to pursue it any further.

PART II

Wherein are Briefly Explained the Principal Questions that Commonly Arise in the Special Field of Metaphysics on God and His Attributes and on the Human Mind

CHAPTER 1

The Eternity of God

Division of Substances

We have already explained that in the nature of things nothing exists except substances and their modes. It will therefore not be expected for us to say anything here about substantial forms and real accidents. For these concepts, and others of the same kind, are totally inept. We have then divided substances into two principal classes, namely Extension and Thought, and Thought into created thought, or the human mind, and uncreated thought, that is, God. Now we have previously proved adequately the existence of God both *a posteriori*, that is, from the idea that we have of Him, and *a priori*, that is, from His essence as the cause of God's existence. But, since we have treated some of His attributes more cursorily than the importance of the subject demands, we have decided to resume them here, and to explain them at greater length, and at the same time to resolve certain problems.

No Duration Belongs to God

The principal attribute that must be considered before all others is the *Eternity* of God, whereby we explain His duration: or rather, to attribute no duration to God, we say that He is eternal. For, as we have noted in Part I, duration is an affection of existence, not of the essence of things. Thus we cannot affirm any duration of God, whose existence is of His own essence. For to attribute duration to God is to distinguish His existence from His essence. There are however some who ask whether God has now not existed longer than since he created Adam. And as this seems quite clear to them, they conclude for that reason that Duration should in no sense be withdrawn from God. But they beg the question. For they assume that the essence of God is distinct from His existence. For they ask whether God, who existed as far back as the creation of Adam, did not add to His existence the time since the creation of Adam to our time. Thus they assign to God a longer duration every single day, and assume that He is continuously as it were self-created. For if they did not distinguish God's existence from His essence, they would in no sense attribute duration to God, since duration can in no manner whatever belong to the essence of things. For no one will ever say that the essence of a circle or a triangle, in so far as it is an eternal truth, has lasted longer now than in the time of Adam.

Furthermore, since duration is conceived as greater or smaller, that is, composed of parts, it manifestly follows that no duration can be attributed to God. For, since His Being is eternal, that is, since nothing before or after can be predicated of Him, we can never affirm duration of Him without at the same time destroying the true concept that we have of God: that is, by attributing duration to Him, we should be dividing into parts what is infinite by its nature and what can never be conceived except as infinite.

Reasons Why Authors Attributed Duration to God

The reasons for the errors made by authors are:

1. That they have attempted to explain eternity without regard to God, as if eternity could be understood without contemplation of the divine essence or as if it were anything other than the divine essence: and that again arises from our having become accustomed, on account of an insufficiency of vocabulary, to attribute eternity to things too whose essence is distinct from their existence: as when we say that there is no contradiction in the world having existed since eternity: and also to the essences of things, while we do not conceive the things as existing: for we then call the essences eternal.

2. Because they did not attribute duration to things except in so far as they considered them to be subjected to a continuous variation, not, as we do, in as much as their essence is   distinct from their existence.

3. Finally, because they distinguished the essence of God, as the essence of created things, from His existence.

These errors, I assert, have been for them an opportunity for new errors. For the first mistake was the reason for their not understanding what eternity was, and for considering it as though it were some aspect of duration.

The second error was their inability to discover readily the difference between the duration of things created and the eternity of God.

Finally, the last error was, since duration is merely an affection of existence, to distinguish the existence of God Himself from His essence and, as we have already said, to attribute duration to God.

What Eternity is

But, to understand more clearly what Eternity is and how it cannot be conceived without the divine essence, what we have already asserted must be considered, namely: that created things, that is, all things except God, always exist solely by the power or essences of God, not by their own power. Hence it follows that the present existence of things is not the cause of their future existence, but only the immutability of God, on account of which we are compelled to say: From the moment that God has created a thing, He will conserve it afterward, that is, He will continue the same action of creation.

Whence we conclude:

1. That a created thing can be said to enjoy existence, because the existence is not of its own essence. But God cannot be said to enjoy existence, for the existence of God is God Himself. So too with His essence.

Whence it follows:

That created things enjoy duration, but God does not do so in any manner whatever.

2. That all created things, while enjoying their present duration and existence, completely lack a future dura-

tion, because it must continuously be attributed to them: but in regard to their essence nothing similar can be predicated. But as for God, since His existence is His essence, we cannot attribute to Him a future existence: for this same existence that He would then have must be attributed to Him in action from this present moment: or, to speak more correctly, infinite existence in action belongs to God in the same way as infinite understanding belongs to Him in action. This infinite existence I term *Eternity,* which is to be attributed to God only, although the duration of these things is unlimited in either direction.

So much for eternity. Of God's necessity I say nothing, because there is no need, since we have proved His existence from His essence. Let us therefore proceed to Unity.

CHAPTER 2

The Unity of God

We have very often been amazed at the futile arguments with which authors try to establish the Unity of God, such as: *If one God could create the world, other gods would be useless. If all things tend to the same end, they have been produced by a single constructor*: and other arguments of a like nature, drawn from external relationships and denominations. Disregarding therefore all these superfluities, we shall here propose our proof as lucidly and briefly as we can, and that in the following manner.

Among the attributes we listed supreme intelligence and we added that He has all His perfection from Himself and not from another. If one now says that there are many gods or many supremely perfect beings, they will all necessarily have to be supremely intelligent. In such a case, it is not sufficient for each one to know only himself. For since each god must know all things, he must know both himself and the other gods. Hence it would follow that the perfection of knowledge of each would depend partly on himself and partly on another god. No god then will be able to be a supremely perfect being: that is, as we have just observed, a being that has all his perfection from himself, not from another. Yet we have already proved that God is a supremely perfect being and that He exists. We can therefore now conclude that He is the unique God in existence. For if many existed it would follow that the most perfect being has an imperfection, which is absurd. So much for the Unity of God.

CHAPTER 3

The Immensity of God

How God can be Said to be Infinite and How, Immense

We have previously explained that no being can be conceived finite and imperfect, that is, participating in Nothing, unless we first consider the perfect and infinite being, that is, God. That is why God alone can be said to be absolutely infinite, since we find that He is composed in reality of infinite perfection. But He can also be called immense or interminable, in so far as we are mindful that no other being exists by whom the perfection of God can be terminated. Hence it follows that the *Infinity* of God, despite the term, is something supremely positive. For we say that He is infinite in so far as we consider His essence or His supreme perfection. But Immensity is ascribed to God only in a relative sense: for it does not belong to God in so far as He is considered absolutely as a supremely perfect being, but in so far as He is considered the first cause. And even if this first cause were not perfect in a supreme degree, but only so in relation to secondary beings, none the less it would be immense. For there would be no being, and consequently no being could be conceived, more perfect than Himself by whom He could be limited or measured. (See more fully on these points *Axiom 9, Part I*).

What is Commonly Understood by the Immensity of God

Often however authors, when discussing the *Immensity* of God, seem to ascribe quantity to God.

For they wish to conclude from this attribute that God must necessarily be present everywhere. As if they wished to say that, if God were not in a certain place, His quantity was limited. This view appears still more clearly from another argument that they adduce to prove that God is infinite or immense (for these two attributes are confused) and also that He is ubiquitous. If God, they declare, is a pure act, as He really is, He is necessarily ubiquitous and infinite. For if He were not ubiquitous, or could not be wherever He wanted to be or had necessarily to move (Note this), it is clearly evident that they attribute *Immensity* to God in so far as they consider Him as a *Quantity*. For they adduce these arguments of theirs from the properties of extension in order to affirm the *Immensity* of God, which is the greatest absurdity possible.

It is Proved that God is Ubiquitous

If one were to ask now how we shall prove *God is ubiquitous,* I reply that this has already been proved and more than adequately by us, when we showed that nothing can exist for even an instant without being re-created by God every single instant.

The Omniscience of Good cannot be Explained

Furthermore, to understand duly the *Ubiquity or Presence of God in every single thing,* it would be necessary to be able to penetrate into the intimate nature of the divine will by means of which He created things and continually re-creates them. Since this transcends human understanding, it is impossible to explain how God is ubiquitous.

Some Consider the Immensity of God Triple, but Wrongly so

Some assert that the *Immensity of God is triple,* namely: immensity of essence, immensity of power, and lastly immensity of presence.

But they are talking nonsense, for they seem to make a distinction between God's essence and His power.

God's Power is not Distinct from His Essence

Others have expressed the same view more openly, declaring that God is ubiquitous by His power, not by

His essence. As if the power of God were distinct from all His attributes, or His infinite essence, whereas it can be nothing else.

For if it were anything else, it would be either a creature, or some accident of the divine essence, without which this essence could be conceived. Both conclusions are absurd. For if it were a creature, it would need God's power for its conservation; and so there would be a succession to infinity.

If it were something accidental, God would not be a being supremely simple, contrary to what has been proved previously.

The Omnipresence of God is Not Distinct either from His Essence

Finally, by Immensity of the presence they also seem to mean something other than God's essence, by which things are created and conserved continuously. Which is certainly a great absurdity into which they have fallen because they have confused God's understanding with human understanding, often comparing His power with that of kings.

CHAPTER 4

The Immutability of God

What Change is and What Transformation is

By *change* we understand in this place the variation that can exist in any subject whatever, with the essence itself of the subject remaining unimpaired; although the term is commonly taken in a wider sense to signify the corruption of things, not indeed an absolute corruption, but one that at the same time involves a subsequent generation: as when we say turf changes into ashes, or that men change into animals. But Philosophers use a different expression to denote this change, namely *Transformation*. But we are here speaking only of the change in which there is no transformation of the subject, as when we say: Peter has changed color, character, etc.

In God Transformation Does not take Place

We must now see whether such changes take place in God: for there is no need to say anything of *transformation*, since we have shown that God necessarily exists, that is, that God cannot cease being, or transform Himself into another god: for in that case He would cease to be and there would be many gods at the same time; which we have shown to be two absurdities.

What are the Causes of Change

To understand more clearly what remains to be said here, we must consider that every *change* proceeds either from external causes, with or without the will of the subject, or from an internal cause, and by the choice of the subject itself. For example, being dark, or sickness, or growing, and such like notions proceed in man from external causes: against the will of the subect or according to his wish: but the desire to walk, to display anger, etc. proceed from internal causes.

God is not Changed by Another Being

The first *changes that* proceed from external causes, do not take place in God. For He alone is the cause of all things, and does not suffer anyone else. In addition, no created thing has in itself any power to exist: and hence much less has it the power of action outside itself or on its own cause. And although we often find in the Holy Scriptures that God was angry or saddened on account of the sins of man, and similar things, the effect is taken in these cases as the cause: as when we say that the Sun is stronger and higher in summer than in winter, although it has neither changed place, nor acquired strength. And that such notions are often taught even in the Holy Scriptures may easily be seen in Isaiah: for he says, chapter 59, verse 2, in rebuking the people: *Your iniquities have separated between you and your God.*

Nor is God Changed by Himself

Let us proceed then and ask whether there can exist in God any change coming from God. This we cannot grant in the case of God; or rather we deny it utterly. For all change that depends on the will of the subject occurs for the purpose of changing his condition for the better: which cannot take place in the supremely perfect being.

Then also a change of this kind does not occur except to avoid some disadvantage with a view to the acquisition of some benefit that is lacking: either of these two suppositions can have no place in God. Hence we conclude that God is an immutable being.

Observe that I have here purposely omitted the ordinary divisions of change, although we have also included them in some way. For there was no need to show each one singly as having no place in God, since we have proved in Proposition 16, Part I that God is incorporeal and that these ordinary divisions comprise only changes of matter.

CHAPTER 5

The Simplicity of God

Three Kinds of Distinction among Things: Real, Modal, Distinction of Reason

Let us proceed to the simplicity of God. To understand rightly this attribute of God, we must recall to mind what Descartes said in his *Principles of Philosophy*, Part I, articles 48 and 49: That there is nothing in the nature of things beyond substances and their modes, from which is deduced the triple distinction (articles 60, 61, and 62), namely: *The Real, the Modal,* and *the Distinction of Reason.* Real distinction is so called when two substances are distinguished from each other, whether they have a different attribute or the same attribute: as, for example, thought and extension, or the parts of matter. The distinction is identifiable from the fact that each substance can be conceived and consequently can exist without the help of the other. *Modal* distinction is shown to be double, namely: that which exists between the mode of a substance and the substance itself: and that which exists between two modes of one and the same substance. And we know this distinction from the fact that, although each mode is conceived without the help of the other, yet neither one is conceived without the help of the substance whose modes they are. This we recognize from the fact that, although the substance can be conceived without its mode, the mode cannot be conceived without the substance. Lastly, a *distinction of Reason* is so called, when it exists between a substance and its attribute: as when duration is distinguished from extension. This distinction is recognized when such a substance cannot be conceived without such an attribute.

The Origin of all Combinations and How Many Kinds of Combination there are

From these three distinctions arises every combination. The first combination is that of two or more substances of the same attribute: as every combination that unites two or more bodies, or of different attribute, as man. The second combination is formed by the union of different modes. Lastly, the third combination is not formed, but is only conceived by Reason as if being formed to produce a readier comprehension of a thing. Things that are not combined in these first two modes must be called simple.

God is Being Supremely Simple

It must therefore be shown that God is not something combined: whence we shall be able to conclude that he is a supremely simple being. And this will be easy to do. For since it is self-evident that the component parts are anterior at least by nature to the combined thing, the substances, by the assemblage and union of which God is composed, will necessarily be by nature anterior to God

Himself and each one will be able to be conceived by itself, without being attributed to God. Then, as these substances are necessarily distinguished from each other in reality, each one of them will also necessarily be able to exist by itself and without the help of the others: and so, as we have just said, there could be as many gods as there are substances, of which God is assumed to be composed. For each, being able to exist by itself, will have to exist of itself: and accordingly will also have the power of assigning to itself all the perfections that we have shown to be in God, and so on: as we have already explained fully in Proposition 7, Part I, where we proved the existence of God. Now since nothing more absurd than this can be uttered, we conclude that God is not composed of an assemblage and union of substances. That in God too there exists no combination of different modes is sufficiently demonstrated from the fact that in God there are no modes. For modes arise from an alteration of the substance (see *Principles, Part I, article* 56). Finally, if anyone wishes to form another combination from the essence of things and their existence, we in no sense contradict him. But let it be remembered that we have now sufficiently proved that these two notions are not distinct in God.

The Attributes of God are Distinguished only by Reason

And hence we can now clearly conclude that all the distinctions that we make among God's attributes are only distinctions of Reason, and that they are not really distinct from each other: by which is understood distinctions of Reason such as I have just mentioned; that are recognized from the fact that such and such a substance cannot exist without such and such an attribute.

159

Hence we conclude that God is a supremely simple being.

With the hodge-podge of distinctions of the Peripatetics we are not concerned: let us therefore pass on to to the life of God.

CHAPTER 6

The Life of God

What Philosophers Commonly Understand by Life

To understand rightly this attribute of God, namely *Life,* it is necessary for us to explain in a general manner what is denoted in everything by its life. And in the first place we shall examine the opinion of the Peripatetics. These philosophers understand by life *the persistence of the nourishing soul with heat* (see Aristotle, *Treatise on Respiration,* Book I, chapter 8). And, since they have imagined three souls, namely: the vegetative, the sensitive, and the intellectual souls, that they attribute only to plants, animals, and men, it follows, as they themselves admit, that other beings are lacking in life.

But yet they did not dare to say that minds and God lack life. Perhaps they were afraid of falling into what is the contrary view of life: If minds and Gods lacked life, they were dead. That is why Aristotle, in his *Metaphysics,* Book II, chapter 7, gives still another definition of life, peculiar only to minds, namely: *Life is the act of understanding.* And in this sense he ascribes life to God, who understands and is pure action. But we shall not exhaust ourselves in refuting these views: for as far as the three souls that they attribute to plants, animals, and men are concerned, we have adequately proved that they are nothing but figments; since we have shown that in matter there are only mechanical assemblages and operations. As for the life of God, I do not know why in Aristotle God is called an act of understanding rather than an act of will and such like. But, expecting no reply to this, I proceed to the explanation of life, as I promised.

To What Things Life may be Attributed

Although this term is often taken metaphorically to signify the character of a man, we shall briefly explain mainly what it denotes philosophically.

It must be observed that, if life is to be attributed to corporeal things too, nothing will be without life. If it is attributed to those beings only in which a soul is united to the body, it will have to be ascribed only to men, or perhaps to animals too; but not to minds or to God. Since however the expression *life* has generally a wider denotation, there is no doubt that it must be attributed to corporeal things too and to minds separated from bodies.

What Life is and What it is in God

We therefore understand by *life the power through which things persist in their being*. And, since that power is different from the things themselves, we rightly say that these things have life. But the power by which God persists in His being is merely His essence. Hence they make a very acceptable assertion when they say that God is life. There are not a few Theologians who be-

161

lieve that for this reason God is life and is not distinct from life. The Jews, when they took an oath, said: *by the living Jehovah,* and not *by the life of Jehovah:* as Joseph, swearing by the life of Pharaoh, said: *By the life of Pharaoh.*

CHAPTER 7

The Understanding of God

God is Omniscient

Among God's attributes we previously enumerated *Omniscience,* which, it is sufficiently established, belongs to God: because knowledge contains a perfection in itself, and God, a being supremely perfect, must lack no perfection. Therefore knowledge must be attributed to God in the highest degree, such as presupposes or implies no ignorance or deprivation of knowledge.

For then there would be an imperfection in the attribute itself, that is, in God. Hence it follows that God never had understanding by power, nor draws any conclusion by reasoning.

Things Exterior to God are not the Objects of God's Knowledge

Furthermore, from the perfection of God it follows that His ideas are not limited, as ours are, by objects situated outside God. But, on the contrary, the things reated by God are determined by God's understanding:[1] or otherwise objects would have by themselves their own nature and essence and would be anterior, at least by nature, to the divine understanding: which is absurd. And certain others, who have not observed this carefully enough, have fallen into grave errors. For some have asserted in fact that there exists a matter outside God, co-eternal with Him, existing by itself, that, according to some, God in his intelligence arranged only in a certain order; while according to others, He imposed certain forms on them besides. Still others have admitted that there are things that, from their nature, are either necessary, or impossible, or contingent, and that for this reason God too knows these things as contingent, and is totally ignorant of whether they are or not. Finally, others have said that God knows contingent things from the circumstances, perhaps because He has had long experience, apart from these I could still mention here other errors of the same kind, did I not consider it superfluous: since the falsity of these opinions becomes self-evident from what has previously been said.

God Himself is the Object of God's Knowledge

Let us therefore return to our proposition, that outside God there is no object of His knowledge, but that He Himself is the object of His knowledge, and that He is even His own knowledge. Those who think that the world is also the object of God's knowledge are far less intelligent than those who propose that an edifice, con-

1. Hence is clearly follows that God's understanding through which He knows created things, and His will and His power, by which He has determined them, are one and the same thing.

structed by some famous architect, be considered as th
object of his knowledge. For the architect is compelle
to seek suitable matter outside himself: but God ha
sought no matter outside Himself, but things, as far a
their essence and their existence are concerned, hav
been produced by His understanding, that is, His wil

How God Knows Sin, and Beings of Reason, etc.

The question is now asked whether God knows evi
and sin, and beings of Reason, and other similar thing
We reply that God must necessarily know those thing
of which He is the cause: especially as they could no
exist even for an instant without the aid of the divin
cooperation. Since therefore evil and sin are not i
things, but only in the human mind that makes com
parisons between one thing and another, it follows tha
God does not know them outside human minds. W
have said that Beings of Reason are modes of thinking
and they must be understood by God in this manner
that is, in so far as we perceive that He conserves an
re-creates the human mind as it has been constituted: no
that God has in Himself such modes of thinking i
order to retain more easily what He knows. And pro
vided attention is paid to the few things that we hav
said, no question will be able to be proposed in regar
to God's understanding that cannot be resolved wit
the greatest ease.

How God Knows Particular Things and How He Know
  Universals

But meanwhile an error must not be passed over in
silence that some make who assert that God knows
nothing except the eternal things, such as angels and

skies, that they have imagined as being by their nature not engendered or corruptible: and, in this world, He knows nothing except species, in as much as they too are non-engendered or corruptible. Those philosophers in fact seem to want to show as it were a particular eagerness in their errors and in imagining the greatest absurdities. For what is more absurd than to take away from God the knowledge of particular things that cannot exist even for an instant without the intervention of God. Then, while asserting that God does not know things that really exist, they attribute to Him in their imagination the knowledge of the universal things that are not and have no essence outside the particular things. We, on the contrary, attribute to God the knowledge of particular things, and deny Him that of the universal things, except in so far as He knows the minds of men.

In God there is only One Idea and a Simple One

Lastly, before we conclude this argument, it seems that a reply should be made to the question whether there are in God many ideas, or only one and that a very simple one. To this I reply that the idea of God, by reason of which He is called omniscient, is unique and very simple. For in reality God is not called omniscient for any other reason except that He has the idea of Himself: this idea or knowledge has always existed at the same time as God, for outside His essence nothing exists, nor could that idea too exist in any other way.

What God's Knowledge is in Regard to Created Things

But God's knowledge in regard to created things cannot properly be related to God's knowledge. For if God had so willed, created things would have had another essence, and this has no place in the knowledge that God has of Himself. It will however be asked whether this knowledge of created things, properly or improperly so called, is multiple or unique. But we reply, this question is in no way different from those that ask whether God's decrees and volitions are many or one: and whether God's ubiquity or cooperation by means of which He conserves every single thing, is the same in all of them: of all which, as we have already said, we can have no distinct knowledge. Still, we know very evidently that, just as God's cooperation, if related to His omnipotence, must be unique, although it is revealed in its effects in different modes, so too God's volitions and decrees (for so it is fitting to call His knowledge in regard to created things), considered in God, are not plural, although they are expressed in different modes through or rather in created things. Lastly, if we consider the analogy of all Nature, we can view it as one Being and consequently the idea or the decree of God in regard to the creation of Nature will be only one.

CHAPTER 8

God's Will

We do not Know how God's Essence and Understanding, by Means of Which He Knows Himself, and His Will, by Means of which He loves Himself, Are Distinguished

God's *Will,* through which He wills to love Himself, necessarily follows from His infinite understanding, by means of which He knows Himself. But how these three notions are distinguished from each other, namely His essence, His understanding, by which He knows Himself, and His will, through which He wills to love Himself, this we set in the sphere of knowledge that we lack. Nor are we unaware of the term (namely *personality*) that Theologians occasionally use to explain the point: but, although we are aware of the term, we still are not aware of its meaning, and we cannot form any clear and distinct concept of it: although we firmly believe that in the most blessed vision of God, promised to the faithful, God will reveal this to His own.

The Will and Power of God, in their External Action, are not Distinct from His Understanding

God's *Will* and *Power* in their external action are not distinct from His understanding, as is sufficiently established from what precedes. For we have shown that God has not only decreed that things should be, but also that they should be of a particular nature, that is, that their essence and their existence must have depended on God's will and power: from which we clearly and distinctly perceive that God's understanding, and His power and will , by which He has created, known, and conserves or loves created things, are in no sense distinguished from each other, but only relatively to our thought.

It is Incorrectly said that God Hates Certain Things and Loves Certain Things

When we say that God hates certain things, and loves certain things, these statements are made in the same sense in which the Scriptures say that the earth will vomit forth men, and other things of this kind. That

God has no anger against anyone and does not love things in the way that the common people believe is a conclusion readily drawn from the Scriptures themselves. For Isaiah says so, and more clearly the Apostle in the *Epistle to the Romans*, chapter 9:

For the children (that is, the sons of Isaac) being not yet born, neither having done any good or evil, that the purpose of God according to election might stand, not of works, but of him that calleth:

It was said unto her, The elder shall serve the younger.

And, somewhat further on:

There hath he mercy on whom he will have mercy, and whom he will he hardeneth.

Thou wilt say then unto me, What, doth he yet find fault? For who hath resisted his will?

Nay but, O man, who art thou that repliest against God? Shall the thing formed say to him that formed it, Why hast thou made me thus?

Hath not the potter power over the clay, of the same lump to make one vessel unto honor, and another unto dishonor?

etc.

Why God Warns Men. Why He does not Save them without Warning: and why the Wicked are Punished

If it is now asked: Why does God warn men? it will be easy to reply that God decreed since eternity to warn men at such and such a time so that those whom He wanted to save could be converted.

If it is still asked: Could God not have saved them without warning? we reply: He could have.

Why then does He not save them? one may perhaps persist in asking.

To this I shall reply when I have said why God did not make the Red Sea passable without a violent east wind and why He does not accomplish every single motion without others: and an infinite number of other actions that God accomplishes by means of causes.

It will again be asked: Why then are the wicked punished? For they act according to their own nature and the divine decree.

I reply that it is also in accordance with the divine decree that they should be punished: and if only those whom we imagine as sinning by virtue of their own freedom were to be punished, why do men try to exterminate poisonous serpents? For they sin only in accordance with their own nature, and cannot do otherwise.

Scripture Teaches Nothing that Contradicts the Light of Natural Reason

Lastly, if other things encountered in the Holy Scriptures induce a doubt in us, this is not the place to explain them: for here we are inquiring only into those questions that we can resolve with the greatest certainty by natural Reason, and it is sufficient to demonstrate these with proof in order to know that the Holy Scriptures must teach the same things. For truth does not contradict truth, nor can the Scriptures teach such nonsense as is commonly imagined.

For if we found something in it that was contrary to the light of Natural Reason, we could refute it with the same freedom as we refute the Koran and the Talmud. But far be it from us to think that in the Holy Scriptures anything can be found that contradicts the Light of Natural Reason.

CHAPTER 9

The Power of God

How the Omnipotence of God is to be Understood

It has already been adequately proved that God is omnipotent. Here we shall only try to explain briefly how this attribute is to be understood. For many speak about it without sufficient piety nor in accordance with the truth. For they say that certain things are possible by their own nature and not in accordance with God's decree; that certain things are impossible, and lastly that certain things are necessary, and that the omnipotence of God takes place only in regard to the possible things. We, however, who have already shown that all things depend absolutely on God's decree, say that God is omnipotent: but perceiving that He has decreed certain things from the mere freedom of His will and secondly that He is immutable we say then that nothing can act contrary to His decree and that this is impossible for the sole reason that it contradicts God's perfection.

All Things are Necessary by Virtue of God's Decree: and Not Some Things in Themselves, and Some Things by Virtue of His Decree

But perhaps some one will object that we find certain things necessary only in regard to God's decree, and others on the contrary without regard to God's decree. For example: Josias burned the bones of the idolaters on the altar of Jerobeam. If we consider only Josias' will, we shall judge the thing as being possible and we shall

170

not say that it must necessarily be so, except that the Prophet had predicted it in accordance with God's decree. But that the three angles of a triangle must be equal to two right angles, the thing itself demonstrates this. But those men imagine distinctions in things through their ignorance. For, if men clearly knew the entire order of Nature, they would find everything as necessary as all those things that are treated in mathematics. But, as this is beyond human understanding, certain things are for this reason judged possible by us, but not necessary. Hence it must be asserted either that God can do nothing since all things are really necessary: or that God can do everything, and that the necessity that we find in things came solely from God's decree.

That if God had Created Differently the Nature of Things, He should also Have given us a Different Understanding

If it is now asked: What if God had decreed things otherwise and had made the things that are now true false, should we not recognize them still as quite true?

Assuredly, if God had left us the nature that He gave us: but if, as He has already done, He had wished to give us such a nature that we should know the nature of things and their laws as they are established by God, that too He would have been able to do: in fact, if we consider His veracity, He ought to have given it. This is also evident from what we have previously said, that all Creative Nature is nothing but a unique being. Hence it follows that man is a part of Nature that must be coherent with the rest.

Therefore it would also follow from the simplicity of God's decree that, if God had created things in another

171

way, He would thereby also have constituted our nature such that we should understand things as they were created by God. For this reason, although we wish to retain the same distinction of God's power that is commonly taught by the Philosophers, we are however obliged to explain it otherwise.

Of How Many Kinds is the Power of God

We therefore divide the *power of God* into *regulated* and *absolute* power.

What is Absolute Power, What is Regulated Power, What is Ordinary, What is Extraordinary

We say that the *power of God* is *absolute,* when we consider His omnipotence without reference to His decrees; *regulated,* when we consider His decrees.

There is furthermore an *ordinary* power and an *extraordinary* power of God. *Ordinary* power is that whereby He conserves the world in a certain order: *extraordinary* is what He uses when He does something outside the order of Nature: as, for example, all the miracles, such as speech given to a she-ass, the apparition of angels, and in similar phenomena. Although there could be grave doubt about this last example, not without reason: for the miracle would seem greater, if God always governed the world in one and the same determined and immutable order than if He abrogated, on account of the stupidity of men, the laws that He Himself excellently established in Nature and by his mere freedom (which cannot be denied by anyone except a person wholly blind). But we leave this decision to the Theologians.

Finally we omit other questions that are customarily raised regarding God's power, namely: *Whether God's power extends to the past: Whether He can do things better than He does: Whether He can do many more things than He has done.*

For these questions can be very easily answered from what has previously been said.

CHAPTER 10

Creation

We have already established previously that God is the creator of all things. Here we shall now attempt to explain what is to be understood by creation: then we shall clarify as far as we can those assertions about creation that are commonly made. Let us begin therefore with the first point.

What Creation is

We say then that *Creation is the operation involving no other causes except the efficient cause, that is, a created thing is one that for its existence presupposes nothing before it except God.*

The Common Definition of Creation is Rejected

It must be observed:

1. That we omit the words *from nothing* that Philosophers commonly use, as if nothing were a matter from which things were produced.

If they express themselves thus, it is due to the fact that, being accustomed, when it is a question of the generation of things, to suppose before these things something *from* which they are made, they have been unable to omit, in creation, the little word *from*. It is the same with them in regard to matter. Seeing that all bodies are in some place and surrounded by other bodies, they have asked themselves where matter was totally contained, and have replied: In some imaginary space.

There is no doubt therefore that, far from considering this *nothing* as a negation of all reality, they have invented or imagined it as something real.

Explanation of the Proposed Definition

2. That I say that in creation no other causes are involved except the efficient cause. I could have said that creation *denies* or *excludes* all causes except the efficient cause. I preferred however to say that no causes *are involved*, to prevent my being compelled to reply to those who ask whether God did not set an end for Himself in creation, in view of which He created things. Moreover, to offer a better explanation, I have added a second definition, namely: A created thing presupposes nothing except God: for, if God set some end of Himself, that end was certainly not exterior to God: for nothing exists outside God by which He is urged to action.

Accidents and Modes are not Created

3. From this definition it follows sufficiently that there is no creation of accidents and modes: for they assume a substance created apart from God.

4. Finally, before creation we cannot imagine any time or duration, but time and duration began with things. For time is the measurement of duration, or rather it is nothing but a mode of thinking. Therefore it presupposes not only whatever thing has been created, but especially thinking men. Now duration ceases when created things cease to be and it begins when created things begin to exist. I say *created things:* for no duration applies to God but only eternity, as we have shown previously with sufficient evidence.

Therefore duration supposes things created before it or at least implies created things. Those who imagine duration and time before created things labor under the same misconception as those who imagine a space beyond matter, as is sufficiently self-evident. So much for the definition of creation.

God's Operation of Creating the World and of Conserving it is the same

Furthermore, there is no need to repeat here once again what we have proved in Axiom 10, Part I, namely: That as much power is required to create a thing as to conserve it: that is, God's operation of creating the world is the same as the operation of conserving it.

After these observations, we shall now proceed to what we promised in the second place.

1. We must therefore inquire what was created, what was uncreated.

2. Whether what was created could be created from eternity.

What Things are Created?

To the first question therefore we reply briefly that all that was created, of which the essence is clearly conceived without any existence, although it is conceived by itself: as, for example, matter, of which we have a clear and distinct concept when we conceive it under the attribute of extension and conceive it with equal clarity and distinctness, whether it exists or does not exist.

How God's Thought Differs from Ours

But someone will perhaps say that we perceive thought clearly and distinctly without existence and still ascribe it to God. But to this we reply that we do not ascribe to God such thought as ours is, that is capable of being affected by things and determined by the nature of things; but thought that is pure act and hence *involving* existence, as we have proved previously at sufficient length. For we showed that God's understanding and His will are not distinguished from His power and His essence, that involves existence.

Outside God Nothing Exists Co-eternal with God

Since therefore all that of which the essence involves no existence must necessarily be created by God in order to exist, and, we have previously frequently expounded, must be continuously conserved by its creator Himself, we shall not linger to refute the opinion of those who have established a world, or chaos, or matter without any form, co-eternal with God, and so independent. We must therefore proceed to the second question and ask: Whether that which was created could have been created from eternity.

The Meaning Here of These Words: from eternity

To understand this properly, we must consider this mode of speaking: *from eternity*: for by this expression we wish to signify at this point quite a different thing from that which we hitherto explained when we spoke of God's eternity. For here we understand nothing more than duration without the beginning of duration, or such a duration that, although we should like to multiply it through many years or myriads of years and this product in turn through other myriads, we should never however be able to express it by any number, however great.

It is Proved that a Thing Could not have been Created From all Eternity

Now it is clearly proved that such duration cannot exist. For, if the world retrogressed from this present moment, it would never be able to have such a duration: therefore the world too could not have appeared since such a beginning up to this present moment.

You will perhaps say that for God nothing is impossible: for He is omnipotent and so will be able to produce the greatest possible duration. We reply that God, because He is omnipotent, will never create duration without the possibility of a greater duration being created. For such is the nature of creation that a greater and smaller duration can always be conceived than a given duration, as in the case of a number.

You will perhaps insist that God has been since eternity, and so has endured to this moment, and so there is a duration such that a greater one cannot be conceived. But in this way duration is ascribed to God consisting of parts, an error that has sufficiently and more than sufficiently been refuted by us, when we proved that eternity, not duration, applies to God. And it would have been good for men to consider this carefully: for they would have been able to extricate themselves very easily from many arguments and absurdities, and, to their great delight, they would have dwelt in the greatest happiest contemplation of this being.

Let us proceed however to answer the arguments adduced by some philosophers, namely by those who try to show the possibility of such infinite duration from the duration that has already passed.

From the Eternity of God it does not Follow that His Effects too can be since Eternity

First of all they assert *that a produced thing can exist at the same time with its cause: now since God has been since eternity, His effects could have been produced since eternity.*

And they support this assertion further *by the example of the son of God, who has been produced since eternity by the father.*

But it is clear to see from what has been said before that they confuse *eternity with* duration, and that they attribute only to God duration since eternity. This is also evident from the example that they adduce. For they assert that this same eternity that they ascribe to the son of God is possible for created things. Moreover, they imagine time and duration before the creation of the world, and propose a duration independent of created things, just as others propose an eternity outside God. It is now evident that both views are as far removed from the truth as possible. We therefore reply that it is utterly false that God can communicate His eternity to creatures: and that the son of God is not a creature but, like the father, is eternal. Thus when we say that the father produced the son since eternity, we mean nothing else than that He always communicated His eternity to the son.

If God Acted from Necessity, He would not Have Infinite Virtue

Their second argument is *that God, when acting freely, has no less a power than when He acts by necessity. But if God acted by necessity, since He has infinite virtue, He would have had to create the world from eternity.*

But this argument too can be very easily answered, if consideration is given to its basis. For these good folk suppose that they can have different ideas of a being of infinite virtue: for they conceive God as having infinite virtue, both when He acts by the necessity of nature, and when He acts freely. We however deny that God has infinite virtue, if He acts by the necessity of nature. This we may now deny: in fact it must be necessarily conceded even by them, after we have proved that a supremely perfect being acts freely, and that only one such can be conceived.

But if they object that it can however be assumed, although it is impossible, that a God acting by the necessity of nature has infinite virtue, we shall reply that it is no more permissible to assume this than a squared circle implying the conclusions that all lines drawn from the centre to the circumference are not equal. And, not to repeat what has been said some time ago, this is quite clear from what precedes. For we have just proved that there is no duration of which the double cannot be conceived, or a duration than which a greater or smaller cannot be conceived: and hence a greater or a smaller duration than a given duration can always be created by God, who acts freely through His infinite virtue. But if God acted through a necessity of nature, this would not follow at all. For only the duration resulting from His nature could be produced by Him and not an infinity of others greater than the given duration. We therefore argue briefly thus: If God created the greatest duration, of such a nature that He could not create a greater one, He would necessarily diminish His power.

But this latter consequence is false, for His power does not differ from His essence. Therefore, and so on. Furthermore, if God acted from the necessity of nature, He would have to create such a duration that He could not create a greater one. But a God creating a duration has not infinite virtue: for we can always conceive a greater duration than the given one. Therefore, if God acted from the necessity of nature, He would not have infinite virtue.

From What we Derive the Concept of a Duration Greater than that of this World

A doubt might here arise in some mind as to how, since the world was created 5000 years ago and more, if the calculation of the Chronologists is correct, we can still conceive a greater duration, that we asserted could not be comprehended without created things.

Such a person can very easily be enlightened, if he takes notice that we know duration not only from the contemplation of created things, but also from the contemplation of God's infinite power to create. For created things cannot be conceived as existing or enduring by themselves, but only by God's infinite power in virtue of which alone they have all their duration. See *Proposition* 12, *Part* I, and its Corollary.

CHAPTER 11

The Intervention of God

Little or nothing remains to be said on the subject of this attribute after we have shown that God continuously creates a thing afresh as it were every single moment. From this we have proved that things never have any power by themselves to perform any act nor to determine themselves for any act: and this takes place in things exterior to man, but also in the human will itself.

Then we also answered certain arguments bearing on this point: and, although many others are usually adduced, still, since they concern Theology particularly, it is my intention here to pass them over. However, as there are many men who admit the intervention of God and take it in a sense altogether different from the one that we have indicated, it must here be observed, with a view to discovering their error very easily, what we proved before, namely: That the present time has no connection with the future (see *Axiom* 10, *Part* I), and that this is clearly and distinctly perceived by us. And if only this is carefully considered, it will be possible to answer without any difficulty all their arguments that can be drawn from Philosophy.

Wherein Consists the Conserving Power of God in the Things that Must be Determined for Action

But, not to touch upon this question idly, we shall answer it in passing. The question is: *Is something added to God's act of conservation when He determines to perform an action?*

When we spoke of motion we already gave an answer to some extent. For we said that God conserves the same amount of motion in Nature. If we therefore consider all material Nature, nothing new is added to the act of conservation: but it may be said in a way that something new is added in respect of particular things. Whether this takes place in spiritual things as well, is not clear: for it does not seem that there is mutual dependence among them. Lastly, as the parts of duration have no connection with each other, we may say that God does not, properly speaking, conserve things so much as He re-creates them. Therefore if a man now has the Fredom determined to perform some act, we must say that God created him thus at that moment. And this is not contradicted by the fact that the human will is often determined by things placed exterior to itself, and that all the things that are in Nature mutually determined to some act: for these things also are thus determined by God.

Nothing can determine a will, and inversely no will can be determined except by the sole power of God. But as for how this does not conflict with human freedom, or how God can achieve this without impairing human freedom, that is something of which we confess ourselves ignorant. On this matter we have already spoken frequently.

The Common Division of God's Attributes is Nominal rather than Real

This is what I had decided to say about God's attributes, among which I have so far established no division. The division that is often described by Authors, who divide God's attributes into incommunicable and communicable, seems to me, to tell the truth, a nominal rather than a real division.

For God's knowledge does not coincide with human knowledge any more than the dog, the heavenly sign, coincides with the dog that is a barking animal, and perhaps God's knowledge resembles human knowledge still less.

The Author's own Division

Now we propose this division. Some attributes of God explain His active essence: others expose nothing of His action, but they do expose His mode of existence.

In this latter category belong unity, eternity, necessity, etc. In the former category belong knowledge, will, life, omnipotence, etc. This division is sufficiently clear and precise, and embraces all the attributes of God.

CHAPTER 12

The Human Mind

We must now pass on to the created substance, that we have divided into extended substance and thinking substance. By extended substance we understood matter or corporal substance. By thinking substance, we understood only human minds.

Angels are not a Matter of Metaphysical but of Theological Consideration

Although Angels too were created, however, not being recognized by the Light of Natural Reason, they do not concern Metaphysics.

For their essence and existence are not known except through Revelation, and so they apply solely to Theology: and the knowledge of Theology, being far different from natural knowledge and totally distinct from it, must not in any way be confused with natural knowledge.

Let no one therefore expect us to say anything about angels.

The Human Mind does not Come from an Intermediary, but is Created by God: but we do not know at what Moment it is so Created

Let us return therefore to human minds, about which only a few things now remain to be said. Only, a warning must be given that we have said nothing about the time of the creation of the human mind, because it is not quite certain at what time God creates it, since it can exist without the body. What is certain is that the human mind does not stem from an intermediary: for that takes place only in things that are generated, as in the modes of a substance: while the substance itself cannot be generated, but only created solely by the Omnipontent Being, as we have adequately proved in what precedes.

184

In What Sense The Human Soul is Mortal

To add something about its immortality, it is quite certain that we cannot say of any created thing that it conflicts with its nature to be destroyed by God's power.

For one who had the power of creating a thing also has the power of destroying it. Furthermore, as we have proved sufficiently, nothing created can exist by its nature even for an instant but is continuously re-created by God.

In What Sense it is Immortal

But, although this is the case, we still see clearly and distinctly that we have no idea by means of which to conceive the destruction of a substance in the way that we have ideas of corruption and the generation of modes. For we conceive clearly, when we consider the structure of the human body, that such and such a structure can be destroyed: but if we consider the corporeal substance, we do not similarly conceive that it can be annihilated. Lastly, the Philosopher does not inquire what the supreme power of God can perform: he judges the Nature of things according to the laws that God has imposed on them: he judges therefore that what is deduced to be fixed and constant according to these laws, is fixed and constant, although he does not deny that God can change these laws and all the rest. For this reason, when we speak of the soul, we do not inquire what God can perform, but only what follows from the laws of Nature.

Proof of the Immortality of the Soul

Since it follows clearly from these laws that a substance cannot be destroyed either by itself or by another created substance, as we have already previously proved abundantly, unless I am mistaken, we are compelled by the laws of Nature to consider the soul as immortal.

And if we want to investigate the subject still more thoroughly we shall be able to prove with the most convincing evidence that the soul is immortal.

For, as we have just shown, it clearly follows from the laws of Nature that the soul is immortal. Now the laws of Nature are the decrees of God revealed by the Light of Natural Reason, as is very manifestly certain from what preceded. Moreover, we have already proved that the decrees of God are immutable. From all these assertions we clearly conclude that God has revealed to men His immutable will regarding the duration of souls, not only by revelation, but also by the Light of Natural Reason.

God does not Act against Nature but above it. What this Act is, according to the Author

We are not refuted by the possible objection that God destroys at any moment these natural laws in order to produce miracles: for most of the wiser Theologians grant that God does nothing against Nature, but acts above it, that is, as I explain, that God has many laws of action that He has not communicated to the human understanding and that, if they had been communicated to the human understanding, would be as natural as the others.

Hence it is most perfectly clear that souls are immortal, and I do not see what remains to be said at this point about the human soul in general.

And there would be nothing further to say especially about its functions, but for the arguments of certain authors, by means of which they try to take it upon themselves not to see and feel what they do see and feel, and which induce me to answer them.

Why Some Think That the Will is not Free

Some believe that they can show that the will is not free, but is always determined by something else. And this belief arises from their understanding by will something distinct from the soul, that they consider as a substance whose nature consists solely in its being indifferent. To remove all confusion, we shall first of all explain the problem and after that we shall very easily discover the fallacies in their arguments.

We have said that the human mind is a thinking thing: whence it follows that solely by its own nature, and considered in itself alone, it can perform any act, namely think; that is, affirm and deny. But these thoughts are either determined by things placed outside the mind, or solely by the mind: since it is itself a substance from whose thinking essence many acts of thought can and must follow. Now it is those acts of thought that have no other cause than the human mind, that are called *volitions*. As for the human mind, in so far as it is conceived as a sufficient cause for producing such acts, it is called the *will*.

Will Exists

That the soul has such a power, although it is not determined by any external things, can be most aptly explained by the example of Buridan's ass. For if we suppose a man instead of an ass in such an equilibrium, the man will have to be considered not as a thinking thing, but as a very stupid ass, if he dies through hunger or thirst. This also follows clearly from the fact that, as we previously stated, we wanted to doubt all things, and not only consider as doubtful those things that can be questioned, but reject them as false. See the *Principles of Cartesian Philosophy,* Part I, article 39.

The Will is Free

It must further be observed that, although the soul is determined to affirm or deny something by external things, it is not however so determined as if it were compelled by external things, but always remains free. For nothing has the power to destroy the essence of the soul: therefore, whatever it affirms and denies, it always affirms and denies freely, as has been adequately explained in the Fourth Meditation.

Hence, if it is asked why the soul wishes this or that, or does not wish this or that, we shall reply:

Because the soul is a thinking thing, that is, a thing that from its nature has the power of willing and not willing, affirming and denying: for it is in this that a thinking thing consists.

Will Must not be Confused With Appetite

After these explanations, let us now examine the arguments of our opponents.

1. The first argument is this: *If the will can will something against the decision of the understanding, if it can desire something contrary to the good prescribed by the last decision of the understanding, it will be able to desire evil by reason of evil. But this conclusion is absurd. Therefore the principle also is absurd.*

From this argument it is clear that they do not understand what the will is: for they confuse it with the appetite that the soul has, after it has affirmed or denied something. This they have learned from their Master, who defined the will as *an appetite by reason of the good.* But we say that the will *consists of affirming or denying that such and such a thing is good,* as we have already previously explained adequately in regard to the cause of error, which we have shown to arise from the fact that the will displays itself more expansively than the understanding.

But if the soul, being free, had not affirmed that a particular thing was good, there would be no appetite. We therefore answer the argument by granting that the soul can will nothing contrary to the last decision of the understanding, that is, cannot will anything in so far as it it suppossed not to will: as is the case here, when it is said that it judged something to be bad, that is, it did not will something.

We deny, however, that it could not absolutely have willed what is bad, that is, judge it to be bad: for that would be contrary to experience itself. For we consider good many things that are bad and, on the other hand, we consider bad many things that are good.

The Will is Nothing But Mind Itself

2. The second argument (or, if one prefers, the first, since there has been no argument so far) is as follows:

If the will is not determined to wish by the last decision of the practical understanding, it will determine itself. But the will is not self-determined, because it is by its nature undetermined.

Hence they proceed to argue thus:

*If the will is of itself and by its nature indifferent
to willing and not willing, it cannot be determined by
itself to will: for what determines must be as determined
as what must be determined is undetermined.*

*But the will, considered as self-determining, is as un-
determined as when it is considered determined. For our
opponents assume nothing in the determining will that
is not also in the will to be determined or that has been
determined; nor is it possible to suppose anything here.
The will therefore cannot by itself be determined to will.
If it is not determined by itself, it is then determined
from another source.*

These are the exact words of Professor Heereboord
of Leyden I, by which he shows clearly that he understands by will not the mind itself, but something else,
outside or inside the mind, something like a *tabula
rasa* cleaned of all thought and capable of receiving any
impression whatever: or rather like a weight in equilibrium that is propelled by another weight in one direction or another, according as this added weight is itself
determined: or, lastly, something that neither himself
nor any other mortal can grasp by any thought.

We have just said, we have even shown clearly, that
the will is nothing but the mind itself, that we call a
thinking thing, that is, affirming and denying. Hence
we clearly deduce that, if we consider solely the nature
of the mind, it has an equal power to affirm and deny.
For that, I assert, is what thinking is.

If therefore we consider, from the fact that the mind
thinks, that it has the power to affirm and deny, why
then do we look for adventitious causes for producing
what follows by its own nature? But, you will say, the
mind itself is not more determined to affirm than to

1. See his *Melemata Philosophica,* second edition, Leyden, 1659.

190

deny: and so you will conclude that we necessarily ought to seek for a cause by which it is determined. But to this I reply with this argument:

If the mind by itself and by its own nature were only determined to affirm (however impossible it might be to conceive this as long as we think of the mind as a thinking being), then by its nature alone it could affirm only, but never deny, however many causes were adduced. But if it is determined neither to affirm nor to deny, it will be capable of doing neither. If, finally, it has either power, as we have just shown to be the case, it will be able solely by its own nature and without any other cause to help it, to do both. This will be clear and certain to all those who consider the thinking thing as a thinking thing: that is, who do not make any distinction whatever, except a distinction of Reason, between the attribute of thought and the thinking thing itself, as our opponents do, who strip the thinking thing of all thought and picture it imaginatively as the first matter of the Peripatetics. This is the manner in which I reply to the argument, and, first, to the major argument: If by will is understood a thing deprived of all thought, we grant that the will by its own nature is undetermined. But we deny that the will is something deprived of all thought and on the contrary we assert that it is thought, that is, power in either sense, to affirm and to deny: by which nothing else can certainly be understood except a cause sufficient for both purposes. Then we also deny that, if the will were undetermined, that is, deprived of all thought, some adventitious cause, other than God by his infinite power to create, could determine it. For to conceive a thinking thing, without any thought, is the same as wanting to conceive an extended thing without extension.

This is one of the early but major works of the Dutch philosopher, in which he interprets to his students the scope and essence of Cartesian thought.

The book is presented in a new translation by Harry E. Wedeck, with a preface by Dagobert D. Runes.